# INSIGHTS
## ON THE BOOK OF
# REVELATION

# INSIGHTS
## ON THE BOOK OF
## REVELATION

### DR. ALAN B. STRINGFELLOW

WHITAKER
HOUSE

All Scripture quotations are taken from the King James Version of the Holy Bible.

Some definitions of Hebrew and Greek words are taken from the electronic versions of *Strong's Exhaustive Concordance of the Bible* (© 1980, 1986, and assigned to World Bible Publishers, Inc. All rights reserved.) or the *New American Standard Exhaustive Concordance of the Bible* (NASC), (© 1981 by The Lockman Foundation. All rights reserved.).

Boldface type in the Scripture quotations indicates the author's emphasis.

**INSIGHTS ON THE BOOK OF REVELATION:**
**A Verse-by-Verse Study**

ISBN: 978-1-64123-094-0
eBook ISBN: 978-1-64123-095-7
Printed in Colombia
© 2018 by Alan B. Stringfellow

Whitaker House
1030 Hunt Valley Circle
New Kensington, PA 15068
www.whitakerhouse.com

7 8 9 10 11 12 13 14 ᕯ 31 30 29 28 27 26 25

# ABOUT PHOTOCOPYING THIS BOOK

# CONTENTS

# PREFACE

This study is designed to be used for as either a formal classroom curriculum or as a person at-home resource. To receive maximum knowledge and inspiration during the next course of study, I offer this encouragement to both the teacher and the student. They are designed to help you become a disciplined disciple of God's Word.

## For the Student

- Read the assigned portion of Scripture at the end of each lesson.
- Take notes on each week's study. Review your notes from the previous week before beginning each study.
- Mark your Bible with key references from one Scripture to another.
- Search the Scripture and mark references in class. Write Scriptures in this book where lines are provided.

Promise the Lord at least two or three hours each week for reading the assigned Scripture and doing your homework. Use the notes section at the end of each lesson to write down any questions that arise while preparing for each lesson. Also, jot down new ideas that are presented during your class time.

The time has come for Christians who mean business for the Lord to devote themselves to the study of His Word in order to master basic biblical principles. Promise yourself and God that you will live up to this standard.

## For the Teacher

If you are teaching this study in a formal classroom setting, first, you must prepare yourself spiritually by reading the book of Revelation in its entirety. These Scriptures will assure you as the teacher that the Holy Spirit will guide you and teach you as you study His Word and impart it to your pupils.

As you teach the course, read the entire chapter or partial chapter assigned for the next lesson. Take notes and search out Scripture references. You must also be prepared to answer questions, add insight, or promise to research answers to any classroom questions you do not know the answer to. What's more, you must...

- Highlight the subject of each lesson.
- Do not be afraid of being too elementary for your pupils.
- Stay on the major themes, not the minor ones.
- Keep the lessons as simple as possible with all age groups.
- Do not change the lesson outline. You may add illustrations and ideas, but do not change the major points of the outline.
- Use your own personality and let the Holy Spirit use you as you teach.
- Expect your pupils to do their part by fully participating in the discussion and rigorously completing assignments.

May God bless you, pupil or teacher, as you begin your study in *Insights on the Book of Revelation*. Let the Holy Spirit teach you both.

# Lesson 1
# INTRODUCTION

No believer's education is complete if he or she does not know the Bible. No believer can live a full and effective life without a firm grasp of the Bible.

## Purpose

Our purpose in this course of study is to provide a solid grounding in the Scriptures on the meaning of the book of Revelation. There is no need to study these outlines and notes *instead* of the Bible. The Bible itself shall be read, searched, and researched as one proceeds through the study.

## Method

We shall study this book, seeking a grasp of controlling thought, the outstanding meaning and message of each chapter, and strive to see it in relation to the whole of God's Word. We must not become so engrossed and fascinated with a subject that we lose sight of the objective: to let the big, broad meanings of the Bible get ahold of us. In each week's study, where lines are provided, please look up the Scriptures and fill in the Scripture or the main truth of the passage.

Let us enter the study reverently, realizing that the Bible is inbreathed by the Holy Spirit, and that He, the Holy Spirit, must be our Teacher. (See John 14:26.)

## The Book of Revelation as a Whole

1. The Book

Our study of this, the last book of the Bible, shall be in twenty-five lessons—one for each of the twenty-two chapters of Revelation, an introduction, an overview of chapters 2 and 3, and a summation of the entire book. We will emphasize the points that:

- God gave to Christ.
- Christ sent by the angel.
- The angel gave to the servant John.
- John gave to the seven churches.

This authenticates every word found in the book of Revelation.

The importance of the book is found Revelation 1:3. There, we find **three beatitudes of the book:**

    a. *"Blessed is he that readeth,…*

    b. *…and they that hear the words of this prophecy,…*

    c. *…and keep those things which are written therein."*

2. The Author

- According to the book itself, the author's name was John (Revelation 1:4, 9; 22:8).
- John was a prophet (Revelation 22:9). He was a leader in the churches of Asia Minor, as indicated in chapters 2 and 3. And he was one of the earliest disciples of the Lord Jesus.
- His family were fishermen and, apparently, they were well-to-do. (See Matthew 4:21.) He, along with James and Peter, had a unique relationship with the Lord. (See Mark 5:37.)
- John is mentioned only three times in the book of Acts (see Acts 3:1; 4:13; 8:14)—and tradition holds that he settled in Ephesus. There, he was later arrested and sent by the Emperor Domitian to the Isle of Patmos, a small island in the Aegean Sea. While there, John received instructions from

the Holy Spirit to write the book of Revelation. It is believed to be one of the last books written in the New Testament.

 * He had already written four other New Testament books: the gospel of John, 1 John, 2 John, and 3 John. In the gospel of John, he reached further back into eternity than any other Bible writer (John 1:1–3). In Revelation, he reaches further into the future than any other Bible writer (Revelation 21, 22). *Man writes history; God writes prophecy.* Revelation is prophecy from God.

3. The Central Message
 * *"The Revelation of Jesus Christ"* (Revelation 1:1).
 * The word *apocalypse* is compounded from a verb and a preposition: *apo-* means "away from," *kalupto* means "to hide, to cover." *Apokalupsis*, therefore, means "to unveil, to reveal."
 * The *"Revelation,"* then, reveals and unveils the coming triumph of Christ.

4. The Structure (Revelation 1:19)
 * *"Write the things which thou hast seen,…"*—chapter 1
 * *"…and the things which are,…"*—chapters 2 and 3
 * *"…and the things which shall be hereafter."*—chapters 4–22

5. The Interpretation
 * Before we get into the verse-by-verse study of Revelation, let me say something about interpretation. This book is a revelation of things that must shortly come to pass. The understanding of when the events of the book will come to pass marks the difference between various schools of interpretation. If we group every theory ever written about this book, we can group them under four general headings. Briefly, they are:

   a. The preterist interpretation
    * *Preterist* is from the Latin word *praeter*, meaning "past." So they are the group who look upon the Revelation as having already been fulfilled in the years and generations of the past.
    * They think that certain chapters of the book of Revelation record the church's victory over Judaism, while other chapters record her victory over Rome. And they think that the entire book was fulfilled by the time of Constantine in A.D. 312.

   b. Historically continuous interpretation
    * These people believe that Revelation is a panorama of the history of the church, from the days of John to the end of the age. They hold that the book has been in process of being fulfilled throughout the whole Christian era.
    * Most of the Reformers interpreted the book in this manner, but every man's interpretation within this viewpoint is a scheme all its own. There is no uniformity of details and there is much dogmatism and contradiction among those who attempt to interpret the book this way.

   c. The spiritualizers—(also called idealists)
    * These people interpret the book as a symbol of the great struggle of good and evil. They do not accept the book as literal—only symbolic.
    * The book of Revelation depicts, according to them, a struggle between the forces of good and the forces of evil, and the ultimate triumph of that which is good.
    * When you spiritualize Scripture, the Bible can be made to mean just about anything you want it to mean. Simply put, the spiritualizers are those who look upon the book as having no distinct meaning at all in time or in history, but merely as a symbolic panorama of the conflict between good and evil. In other words, it seems to be only an allegory.

d. The futurist interpretation
- This is the group who believe that beginning at the fourth chapter of Revelation, an unveiling of the consummation of the age is described.
- Most of us who are called "evangelicals" believe this basic interpretation—that most of the things in this book are yet to come to pass. So we call ourselves futurist because, in this book of Revelation, we follow the things that lead up to that great final consummation, the establishment of the kingdom of our Lord on the earth, and we even have a record of the new heaven, the new earth, the new Jerusalem, and our eternal home with God.
- Those of us who believe this way find two or three things that make us believe that the book of Revelation must be interpreted this way:
  1.) Most of the things that are written in the book of Revelation have never been fulfilled. They are still to be seen; they are still to come to pass. There have never been, in the history of humanity, such judgments as you find recorded in the book of Revelation.
  2.) Revelation speaks of resurrections that are yet to come to pass. God's people are going to be raised from the dead. They are going to be given a part in the kingdom of Jesus. God's saints are going to be with Him at the marriage supper of the Lamb. The wicked dead are going to stand at the white throne of the judgment of God.
- In other words, all of this is in the future. Therefore, we are called *futurists* and we start from the premise that we have not seen the rapture of the church—because we are still here—and that the tribulation is still in the future—because the church is still here.

Nothing in history can compare to the judgments depicted in this book.

*I would encourage you to withhold deciding on which theory you might agree with until after you have finished this course of study.*

6. Attitudes Toward Revelation
- Generally speaking, there are two extreme attitudes toward Revelation.
  a. Some say the book cannot be understood, and therefore, it should not be studied, taught, or preached. Differences of interpretation, they point out, have divided Christians and therefore should not be interpreted.
  b. Others consider themselves so sure of every detail of the book that they set dates and propose drastic interpretations of the book.
- The proper attitude toward this book does not lie in either extreme. The book is important and profitable, as is all Scripture.
- *We must approach it with the sense of total dependence upon the Holy Spirit as our teacher.* Even though this book is largely about the future, knowledge of it should affect our living in the present.
- Its study helps to answer many questions about other portions of Scripture that seemingly would be hard to interpret without some knowledge of the book of Revelation.

7. From Genesis to Revelation
- The book of Revelation is the completion of the circle of the revealed Word of God. What is begun in Genesis finds its concluding and consummating climax in the Revelation.
- Genesis provides the story of the creation of the heavens and the earth; Revelation is the story of the creation of the new heaven and the new earth.

- In Genesis, we read of man losing his first paradise. In Revelation, we read of how paradise is returned to the fallen man.

- Genesis gives the story of the tree of life and how man was driven from it. In Revelation, it is the story of the tree of life and how man is invited back to it.

- In Genesis, we are introduced to Satan for the first time; in Revelation, he appears for the last time in his ultimate and certain doom.

- In Genesis is the story of the entrance of sin into the world—with the sorrow and toil and heartache it brings. The book of Revelation describes the great announcement that *"there shall be no more sorrow nor crying; neither shall there be any more pain"* (Revelation 21:4).

- In Genesis is the story of the first death, the first mound of earth heaped up, over which the first parents wept and cried. In Revelation, there is the glorious announcement that says *"that there shall be no more death"* (Revelation 21:4).

- Genesis tells of the story of man's vast disobedience and of the building of the tower of Babel. Revelation is the story of the destruction of Babylon, and the world system that it represents.

- In Genesis, there is the story of the creation of the first man, Adam, and his dominion over all things that God made. In Revelation, there is the story and the revelation of the second Adam, and His dominion over things in heaven and in earth.

- In Genesis is the story of the first woman, the first bride, and how she was made a help mate for the man. In Revelation, there is the story of the bride, the church of Christ, and how she shall share with Him in His great and exalted eternal glory.

## How Much Do You Remember?

1.  Name the books John the Apostle wrote.
2.  What is the central message of Revelation?
3.  Where was this book written?
4.  What is the structure of the book?
5.  What are the four general interpretations of this book?
6.  What is the correct way to approach this book while avoiding extreme attitudes?
7.  Recount three ideas from the book of Genesis that are brought full circle in Revelation.

## Your Assignment for Next Week:

1.  Read Revelation 1.
2.  Review your notes from this introduction.
3.  Underline and mark your Bible.

## Lesson 1 Notes

_____

_____

_____

_____

_____

_____

_____

_____

_____

_____

_____

_____

_____

_____

_____

_____

_____

_____

_____

# Lesson 2
# REVELATION 1

1. *"Write the things which thou hast seen…"* (Revelation 1:19).

  - In obedience to that command, John began in chapter 1 to write down the things that he had seen. He saw the glorified Lord, the Alpha and the Omega, the beginning and the ending.

2. The Introduction of the Chapter (verses 1–2)

  a. *"The Revelation of Jesus Christ"*

    - *"Revelation"* comes from the Greek word *apokalupsis*, or apocalypse, which means a revealing or unveiling. This is a revealing or unveiling of the Lord, Jesus Christ.

  b. *"which God gave unto him, to shew unto his servants"*

    - Here, the reason for this revealing is made clear, so that the Revelation would be made known, not hidden.

    - We see the unusual words, *"which God gave unto him."* God has, in covenant, made a promise to our Lord, Jesus Christ. Because Christ humbled Himself, because He poured out His life unto death, and because He became flesh and blood and suffered for the sins of the world, God has given to Him a great reward. The fullness and glory of that reward are seen in the pages of Revelation.

    - Because our Lord humbled Himself and suffered for our sins, God, in covenant, has declared that He will exalt our Savior above all principalities, powers, and authorities.

  c. *"which must shortly come to pass"*

    - Here we are given a timeframe for the Revelation. These things are eminent and will happen within a short amount of time, but have not yet occurred.

    - How soon is *"shortly"*? Keep in mind that this is God's timeframe, not man's. The time of fulfillment may seem distant, but when it does come, there will be no delay in its execution—and events will transpire rapidly.

  d. *"and he sent and signified it by his angel unto his servant John."*

    - Both the method of delivery of the Revelation and the author of the book are made known.

    - Notice how the communication was transmitted: God, the Father; to Christ; to an angel; to John; to God's servants. John was the human instrument who testified of the Word of God and the testimony of Christ, as seen in the following verse.

  e. *"Who bare record of the word of God, and of the testimony of Jesus Christ, and of all things that he saw."*

    - In this introduction, we see that John knew that he was writing Holy Scripture.

3. Symbols of the Chapter

  - As we look at the first verse, we find the word *"signified."* Let us pronounce this word as it is spelled: *sign-ified*. The angel was able to pass before the eyes and in the presence and hearing of John on the Isle of Patmos. The angel gave to John the things that are yet to come. John saw them and they were *sign-ified*. In other words, John saw them by signs and symbols. It is the same kind of thing that Satan did for Jesus when he took our Lord upon a high mountain and showed Him all the kingdoms of the world and the glory of it in only a moment.

- The angel caused to pass before John's eyes all of these things that are to come in the ages that are to follow.
- The symbols in that word *"signified"* represent many different things, because in this book, we find that it portrays angels and demons, powers and principalities, and agents and nations and potentates. We will find that many of these symbols and signs are explained and you can usually find their meaning in the apocalyptic and prophetic words of the Old Testament, as well as the new. We will cover many examples of this as we study the book of Revelation.

4. The Three Beatitudes of Revelation
   - The importance of this book can be found in chapter 1 verse 3. Look up this verse:

   _____

   _____

   _____

   - God says that we are blessed by reading the book and for guarding and treasuring the words of this prophecy.
   - Remember that this book is unsealed and that John was instructed not to seal up the book. God has given us the unsealed book that our eyes may look upon it and our hearts may be strengthened by it.

5. The Salutation (1:4)
   - Here, John addresses the letter to the seven churches that are in Asia—we shall cover these seven churches in chapters 2 and 3.
   - John extends the salutation in the name of the trinity.
   - John extends the salutation by writing a descriptive trinity of the first person of the Godhead—the Lord God—when he says, *"which is, which was, and which is to come."*
   - He writes a descriptive trinity of the third person of the Godhead: *"seven Spirits which are before his throne"* (1:4).
   - As he had three things to say about the other two persons of the Godhead, so he says three things about Jesus, our Lord, *"who is the faithful witness, and the first begotten of the dead, and the prince of the kings of the earth"* (1:5).
   - The salutation, therefore, is in the name of the triune God, *"which is, and which was, and which is to come"* (1:4); from the Holy Spirit, described as the seven Spirits of God—representing the seven-fold ministry of the Spirit as described in Isaiah 11:2—and from Jesus Christ, who is the faithful Witness and the first begotten of the dead and the Prince of the kings of the earth.

6. A Glorious Ascription of Praise
   - In the middle of verse 5, we find John giving this praise to our Lord:
     *"Unto him that loved us, and washed us from our sins in his own blood, and hath made us kings and priests unto God and his father; to him be the glory and dominion for ever and ever. Amen."*
   - It seems as though while John was dictating the mind of the Holy Spirit, when he came to mention the name of Jesus, he arose and knelt in adoration and in glory.
   - The things John mentions in this ascription of praise are things concerning our salvation: First, *"Unto him that loved us."* Second, unto Him who *"washed us from our sins in his own blood."* Third, we see the result—unto Him who *"hath made us kings and priests unto God and his father."*
   - More of these doxologies and ascriptions of praise are found throughout the book of Revelation. (See also Revelation 4:9–11; 5:13; 7:11–12.)

- The spontaneity of this ascription of praise is like that of the rest of the apostles, as Paul mentioned in Ephesians 3:20–21.

- Look up Ephesians 3:20–21:

_____

_____

_____

_____

_____

- Similar ascriptions of praise can be found in 1 Timothy 1:17 and Jude 1:24–25.

- Briefly, to get a glance back in verses 4 and 5 we have a greeting from the Trinity: the Father; seven Spirits, representing the sevenfold ministry of the Spirit, as depicted in Isaiah 11:2; and Christ, designated as the faithful Witness, the First Born from the dead (His resurrection), and the Ruler (not prince) of the kings of the earth, which refers to His future rule over the earth. The book is dedicated to Christ, who was its author, and about whom it speaks. Three things are ascribed to Him in verses 5 and 6:

    a. First, He loves us (present tense).

    b. Second, He loosed us, washed us, from our sins in His blood.

    c. Third, He made us a kingdom (not kings) and priests of God. The word *kingdom* views believers as a body, or corporately in our relationship with Christ, while the word *priests* refers to our individual relationship with Him.

7. The Theme and the Text of the Book of Revelation—verse 7

- This is the cry we read throughout the Word of God, and especially in this book of Revelation. The grand announcement: *"Behold, he cometh with clouds; and every eye shall see him"* is the subline recurring theme of the entire Bible. Here are examples of these reoccurrences that tell of Christ's coming:

    a. In the garden of Eden, the promise of the Lord that the seed of the woman would bruise the serpent's head, found in Genesis 3:15, is nothing more than this same glorious proclamation: *"Behold, he cometh."*

    b. Matthew 24:37: *"But as the days of Noah were, so shall also the coming of the Son of man be."* The trials and sorrows, the psalms and songs of David, are mere prototypes of the return of our Lord.

    c. In the New Testament, one out of every twenty verses concerns the Second Advent of the Lord Jesus Christ.

    d. In Luke 19:13, Christ says to the ten servants, *"Occupy till I come."*

    e. In John 14:1–3, the Lord comforts His disciples, and He did so with words about His coming again when He said, *"Let not your heart be troubled…. If I go…I will come again, and receive you unto myself."*

    f. Paul preached the same theme about the coming of Christ. In 1 Corinthians 15:51–52, Paul says, *"I shew you a mystery; we shall not all sleep, but we shall all be changed, in a moment in the twinkling of an eye, at the last trump: for the trumpet shall sound, and the dead shall be changed."*

    g. Philippians 3:20–21, *"For our conversation is in heaven; from whence also we look for the Saviour, our Lord Jesus Christ: who shall change our vile body, that it may be fashioned like unto his glorious body."*

h.  Another example is the entire substance of the letter to Thessalonica, of which every chapter ends with a discussion of the return of our Lord.

i.  In Titus 2:13, Paul says, *"Looking for the blessed hope, and the glorious appearing of our great God and our Saviour Jesus Christ."*

j.  Hebrews 9:28 says, *"Unto them that look for him shall he appear the second time without sin unto salvation."*

k.  And Jude 14: *"Behold, the Lord cometh with ten thousand of his saints."*

+  So you see that this is the summary and the climactic theme of the glorious text of the whole Bible: *"Behold, he cometh with clouds; and every eye shall see him"* (Revelation 1:7). Take this promise out of the Christian faith and you have a mutilated fragment of the Word of God. As He went away, so shall He return. Surely, His feet shall rest upon the summit of the Mount of Olives. If he went away for our justification, He shall return for our redemption and our ultimate, full salvation.

8.  The Announcement: *"Behold, he cometh with clouds."*

+  John was present when our Lord went away. He saw the clouds receive Him out of his sight, and he heard also the angel's announcement recorded in Acts 1:11: *"This same Jesus, which is taken up from you into heaven, shall so come in like manner as ye have seen him go into heaven."*

+  Always, when our Lord is presented as appearing and as coming again, it is with clouds. Look at these few examples:

a.  Daniel 7:13: *"I saw in the night visions, and, behold, one like the Son of man came with the clouds of heaven, and came to the Ancient of days."*

b.  Matthew 24:30: *"And then shall appear the sign of the Son of man in heaven: and then shall all the tribes of the earth mourn, and they shall see the Son of man coming in the clouds of heaven with power and great glory."*

c.  Matthew 26:62, 64: *"And the high priest arose, and said unto him, Answerest thou nothing? what is it which these witness against thee?... Jesus saith unto him, Thou has said: nevertheless I say unto you, Hereafter shall ye see the Son of man sitting on the right hand of power, and coming in the clouds of heaven."*

+  To those of us who love the Lord, we now know that there is no meaning to the first coming of our Lord if we forget the second. The first coming is without significance except for the glorious consummation in the Second Advent.

9.  A Secret and Open Coming—verse 7

+  I present this at this time because it seems that there is a contradiction here in Scripture. Let's study this to find out using Revelation 1:7, along with other verses from the Bible.

a.  A secret coming

+  Revelation 16:15 says, *"Behold, I come as a thief. Blessed is he that watcheth, and keepeth his garments, lest he walk naked, and they see his shame."*

+  Revelation 3:3: *"I will come on thee as a thief, and thou shalt not know what hour I will come upon thee."*

+  Matthew 24:42 reads similarly, saying, *"Watch, therefore: for ye know not what hour your Lord doth come."*

+  First Thessalonians 5:2 says, *"For yourselves know perfectly that the day of the Lord so cometh as a thief in the night."*

Now is this a contradiction? No! For you see, when we read the text in Revelation 1:7, we must read exactly what the Spirit of God has said, not what we *think* He said.

Look up Revelation 1:7, and ponder exactly what it says:

_____

_____

_____

_____

It does not say, as so many infer, that all shall see Him at the same time, in the same place, in the same manner, and with the same feeling. There will be some who will see Him when He comes as a thief to steal away His jewels—meaning us. There will be some who will see him as the terrible lightening breaks open the sky and He comes in all of His judgment.

    b.   An open coming

- *"And they also which pierced him…all kindreds of the earth shall wail because of him"* (Revelation 1:7).
- Those who drove the nails into His hands and thrust the spear into His side shall someday confront the Lord, face to face.
- The word *"kindreds"* here means "tribes." This includes all of the families of the earth.
- The church has been called out, and here, in the world, we see the rejection and the unbelievers, and then the great judge of the world appears. In a moment, how the earth changes because of the judgment of God.

- There are two acts in this great, final, climactic drama: He is coming as a thief to steal away His people, the church; He is also coming upon the throne of His glory and of His judgment.
- All must someday look upon the face of the Lord Jesus. So there are two ways that our Lord is to come—first, secretly, as a thief unannounced coming for His people. Then, He is coming into this earth with His saints, that is us, as lightening, visible where every eye of the unbelieving shall see Him—establishing, in this world, a final mandate of peace and the establishment of the millennial kingdom of our God.

10.  I Am—verse 8

- *"I am Alpha and Omega."*
- *Alpha* is the first letter of the Greek alphabet; *omega* is the last. Christ is claiming that He is everything, from beginning to end, from a to z.
- Two major attributes of Christ are emphasized in these opening comments of Revelation

    a.   *"Which is, and which was, and which is to come"* (verse 4). This conveys the idea that Christ existed before any specific point in time, and that He will continue to exist after time gives way to eternity.

    b.   *"The Almighty"* (verse 8). This literally means "the omnipotent and all powerful one."

These attributes can only be true of someone who is God. There is no limit to the power of the Almighty Christ.

11.  *"In the isle that is called Patmos"*—verse 9

- John tells us some important things in this verse.
- He identifies himself.
- He shows his relationship to other believers when he says, *"I John, who also am your brother, and companion in tribulation"* (Revelation 1:9).

- John was not on the Isle of Patmos because he was old; he was sent there because he preached the Word of God with zeal.

- John would not bow down to any ruler or image, namely the Roman Caesar Domitian, so he was exiled to the Isle of Patmos.

- Patmos is only about twenty-five miles in diameter and is very rugged and mountainous. John was not chained, guarded, or cast into a dungeon. It was in this setting that he saw the sublime Revelation.

- Why does the Lord permit His people to be persecuted and suffer? God has an elected purpose in these sorrows and trials. Out of them, His truth is made known to the world.

- As you look at verse 9, you would think that John would have been defeated in his circumstances. I am sure that most of us would have felt sorry for ourselves, but John was in the Spirit and was on the Isle of Patmos for a purpose. The reason he was there can be found in this verse of study: *"For the word of God, and for the testimony of Jesus Christ"* (verse 9).

12. A Glorified Vision of the Lord Jesus—verses 10–16.

- Here, we take a section of Scripture that presents a vision of the Lord Christ. The first and most important thing that John saw in his Patmos vision was Christ Himself.

- Remember that John was in the Spirit on the Lord's Day.

- The commandment came with the voice of a trumpet, a harbinger in the Bible for important messages, happenings, and revelations.

- With the voice of the trumpet, John is commanded to write these things for the people of God:

  a. *"What thou seest, write in a book, and send it unto the seven churches which are in Asia"* (1:11).

    - John sees Christ standing then in the middle of the seven golden lamp stands, which symbolize the seven churches he is addressing.

    - These lamp stands were in the likeness of those who provided all the light of the ancient Jewish tabernacle.

    - This picture of Christ, standing in the middle of the lamp stands, presents Him as the Light of the world, illuminating mankind to the true meaning of God.

    - John names the seven churches he is to send his writings to: Ephesus, Smyrna, Pergamos, Thyatira, Sardis, Philadelphia, and Laodicea.

    - These were the seven churches of Asia, connected by ancient Roman roads over which the messenger carrying the document could easy make the journey from one church to another.

    - Why only seven churches when there are many more churches in Asia? The number seven, according to its symbolic meaning in Scripture, represents the whole, the complete. It is a full and completed number. When Christ addresses the messages to the seven church of Asia, He addresses all of the churches of all ages and of all times.

  b. *"And I turned to see the voice that spake with me. And being turned, I saw seven golden candlesticks; and in the midst of the seven candlesticks one like unto the Son of man"* (verse 12).

    - This is to say, "I saw in the midst of the seven lamp stands the seven churches—one like unto the Son of man."

    - John had not seen the Lord for over sixty years.

    - The last time he saw Him, He was ascending up into heaven.

    - First, he saw the humanity, the human form of God, the Son of man. The Son of man, God in humanity—God incarnate.

    - Yet he says, *"one **like** unto the Son of man."* The description that follows is beyond what we could ever describe. But that figure that John saw in His glory is the Alpha and the Omega, the beginning and the ending, which was, which is, which is to come, the Almighty, the Lord God—God Himself.

c.   A description of our Lord

   • John described the vision of the living Lord. Look up Revelation 1:13–16:

_____

_____

_____

_____

_____

_____

_____

_____

_____

_____

_____

_____

   • John presents the Lord with two symbols of function and seven symbols of character.

The symbols of **function** are:

1.) *"clothed with the garments down to the foot"* (1:13)

   • This refers to His dignity, His judicial authority, and His kingly presence.

   • He was clothed with a garment down to the foot, the priestly dress of a priest and the regal robes of a king.

2.) *"and girt about the paps with a golden girdle"* (1:13)

   • This is from that ancient time when a man was to serve, when he was to run or to work, he girded up his loins. But this girdle is about his breast. He is in kingly repose of the Son of God, who sets down upon the throne of the Almighty.

   • This symbol also refers to His affection, His understanding, His sympathy, and His love for the people of the Lord.

The symbols of **character** are:

1.) *"His head and his hairs were white like wool, as white as snow"* (1:14)

   • This refers to the purity of His thoughts and the eternity of His character as "the Ancient of Days." It is eternal dignity.

2.) *"and his eyes were as a flame of fire"* (1:14)

   • This indicates the omniscience of the almighty God.

   • Hebrews 4:13 says, *"but all things are naked and open unto the eyes of him with whom we have to do."* His eyes are like a burning flame.

3.) *"and his feet like unto fine brass"* (1:15)

- All of the instruments in the outer court were made of brass because they had to do with judgment. *"His feet like unto fine brass, as if they burned in a furnace."*

- No man can look upon the holy righteousness of the presence of God. He treads upon his enemies; He walks upon sin.

4.) *"and his voice as the sound of many waters"* (1:15)

- *"Many waters"* refers to many messengers—many prophets, although there is but one great eternal Word of the Lord.

- As a mighty river is gathered from many streams and many sources, so His voice is as a sound of many, many waters.

- Many waters, but one great voice.

5.) *"And he had in his right hand seven stars"* (1:16)

- The seven stars are translated seven angels, messengers, or pastors of the seven churches.

- In the hand of authority—His right hand, which is the hand of might, skill, strength, and power—God holds up and holds out His servants.

- The preacher is a messenger, and he is also a star reflecting the light of the glory of God. The minister does not create the light but he reflects the light of the Son of God.

6.) *"and out of his mouth went a sharp twoedged sword"* (1:16)

- The two-edged sword is the Word of God. This is the power of the delivered message of Christ.

- Ephesians 6:17 says, *"The sword of the Spirit…is the word of God."*

- The Word of God is the living, burning judgment of the Almighty upon the world.

7.) *"and His countenance was as the sun shineth in his strength"* (1:16)

- The stars are the preachers of the Word, but Christ is the power, the glory, and the triumph, and His countenance was as the sun shining.

- On the road to Damascus, Saul of Tarsus met Christ. He saw that face, and the countenance on His face as the sun in the brightness of the noon day.

- In 2 Corinthians 4:6, Paul says, *"For God, who commanded the light to shine out of darkness, hath shined in our hearts, to give the light of the knowledge of the glory of God in the face of Jesus Christ."*

13. The Lord Who Is Alive—verse 17

- *"And when I saw him, I fell at His feet as dead"* (1:17).

- This was a reverential awe of John before the Lord Christ.

- He is looking upon the Ancient of Days and sees those seven things he has described in the previous verses, and he falls down before the Lord as one who might be dead.

- Being overpowered by the vision of the glorious Lord, we read that sweet verse which says, *"he laid his right hand upon me, saying unto me, Fear not"* (1:17).

- Notice the right hand, the hand of favor, and the hand that supports weakness, lifting up the fallen and giving strength to those who have no strength.

- He didn't have to make the gesture. He could have just spoken to John, but this is like our Lord. Christ always put His hand upon the eyes of the blind and the ears of the deaf. He would heal the sick by touching them.

14. The Keys of the Lord Jesus Over Hell and Death—verse 18

   - Notice how Christ describes Himself at the end of verses 17 and 18: *"I am the first and the last: I am he that liveth, and was dead; and, behold, I am alive evermore, Amen; and have the keys of hell and of death."*

   - This verse testifies to the universal lordship of Christ.

   - His sovereignty is presented likewise in Philippians 2:9–11:
   *Wherefore God also hath highly exalt him, and given him a name which is above every name: that at the name of Jesus every knee should bow, of things in heaven, things in earth, and things under the earth; and that every tongue should confess that Jesus Christ is Lord, to the glory of God the Father.*

   - Jesus as Lord is king over all. It is said here in these words: *"I…have the keys of hell and of death."* This could be and should be termed as follows: "I have the keys of Hades (men's souls) and of the grave (men's bodies)."

   a. Look at the authority of Christ over the unseen world.

      - The keys are a symbol of authority, control, and possession.

      - Isaiah prophesied in Isaiah 9:6, *"and the government shall be upon his shoulder."*

      - As terrible as they are, the powers of hell and of death are not allowed to run riot without authority and control. There is nothing in heaven or under heaven, nothing in earth or under earth, and nothing in life or in death that is not under the surveillance of the great God and our Savior, Jesus Christ.

   b. Let's look at the term "keys of Hades."

      - That is, Christ is ruler of the unseen world—the world of men's *souls*. (The difference between spirit and soul: spirit is always un-incarnate, or always spirit. Soul carries with it the idea of a body without exception. Spirit can be pure spirit, unassociated from the body, but soul is always associated with the body. We talk about Christ being the king over the souls of men because the body shall be a part of the redemptive plan of God. When I say soul, I am referring to the believer, whose body is in the grave and whose spirit is with the Lord, still looking forward to that great glorious day when God shall reunite the souls of men with the bodies that are now in the heart of the earth.)

      - Christ is adored in heaven and feared in hell.

      - You can paraphrase this verse as the Lord saying, "I have the keys of heaven, and of glory, and of paradise, and no one can pluck them out of my hand." We are safe forever and eternally.

   c. What about the keys of hell?

      - He also has the key of torment, of Gehenna. This place is called torment, damnation, and perdition.

      - When we die, we are with our Lord in paradise, in glory, but when the damned or the lost die, they fall into perdition or damnation.

      - Our Lord is king over hell. The lost and damned would not recognize or believe Him in this life, so now, in the life to come, they bow and they confess in torment and in agony.

      - When a soul goes beyond the convicting power of mercy and grace and passes away, that key is turned, and it is turned forever. Only Jesus has the key. This key shall someday be turned on Satan.

d. The keys of death.

Now we discuss men's bodies fallen into the grave.

- Death is a horrible spectacle. God calls death an enemy. Death is an intruder.

- None of us escape death because by one man, sin came into the world, thereby by one man we shall die.

- But the Lord Jesus says, *"I...have the keys of hell and of death."* The key is in His hand.

- When you die is known to Him. How you die is known to Him.

- Death, to the Christian, is not death; we fall asleep in Jesus. In death, we wait with the Lord for that great and final consummation and full redemption of the purchased possession, which is soul and body.

- We are not to be afraid, for to us, death is being with our Lord.

- Christ shall reign over death and we shall be raised incorruptible.

- Look up 1 Corinthians 15:25–26:

_____

_____

_____

_____

15. God's Outline of the Apocalypse—verse 19.

- This particular part of the lesson is key to the interpretation of the book of Revelation. The text is God's outline, which can't be beat. There are many man-made outlines, and all of them sound good, but none are God's own outline for us.

a. In verse 19 you find the outline: *"Write the things which thou hast seen."* That's the first part.

- This is the first division of the book. In obedience to that command, John sat down and wrote the things he had seen (the seven lampstands, the vision of the living Lord, all recorded in chapter 1)

b. The second part of the outline is *"write...the things which are"* (1:19).

- He is talking about the churches, which is found in Revelation 1:20: *"the seven candlesticks which thou sawest **are** the seven churches."*

- So the second great division of Revelation concerns the things of the seven churches—all the churches down through the ages, which you will find in Revelation 2 and 3—the second part of the outline.

c. The third part of the outline says, *"write...the things which shall be hereafter."* These things are after these churches. (1:19)

- The third part of the outline begins in the fourth chapter of Revelation and continues through the end of the book.

- Here, John discloses what God is going to do in His judgment upon this world after the church has completed its history, and after Christ has come for us.

- When we turn to the fourth chapter of the book of Revelation, the church is gone. The next time we meet the church is in chapter 19 of Revelation, as the bride at the marriage supper of the Lamb.

- In the last verse of chapter 1, God Himself explains the symbolism of the seven stars and seven candlesticks or lampstands. God sets an encouraging pattern here by showing that all of the symbols in the book of Revelation have meaning.

- This concludes John's writings of the first part of Revelation, in which he describes the things which he has seen. In the next lesson, we will begin part 2 of God's outline for Revelation, in which John describes the *"things which are."*

## How Much Do You Remember?

1. What does the word *"Revelation"* mean?
2. What is the chain of communication in the delivery of the Revelation?
3. What are the three beatitudes of Revelation?
4. What is the theme of the book of Revelation that also reoccurs throughout the Bible?
5. How is our Lord always presented as coming and appearing?
6. How will Christ's coming be secret *and* open?
7. What do the seven lampstands symbolize?
8. Describe the vision John has of the Lord Jesus from verses 10–16.
9. Explain what it means when we read that Christ has the keys to hell and death.
10. What is the structure or outline of Revelation, given by God in verse 19?

## Your Assignment for Next Week

1. Read Revelation 2 and 3.
2. Review your notes from this lesson.
3. Underline and mark your Bible.

## Lesson 2 Notes

_____

_____

_____

_____

_____

_____

_____

_____

_____

_____

_____

_____

_____

_____

_____

_____

_____

_____

# Lesson 3
# AN OVERVIEW OF REVELATION 2–3

1. *"What thou seest, write in a book, and send it unto the seven churches which are in Asia"* (Revelation 1:11).
   - Revelation 2 and 3 unfold these seven churches.
   - The seven churches represented in these chapters are actual churches.
   - We shall understand some of the meanings of the seven churches as we progress through this lesson.
2. *"These things saith he that holdeth the seven stars in his right hand, who walketh in the midst of the seven golden candlesticks"* (Revelation 2:1).
   - The angels of the seven churches are messengers—those who are entrusted with communication.
   - A messenger is called "a star" because he is an illuminator.
   - The seven candlesticks are the seven churches, as we read in Revelation 1:20.
3. The Symbolic Meaning of the Seven Churches of Asia
   - The seven churches also are representative of all the churches of Christ throughout past, present, and future history. We know this is true because of five reasons:
     a. The number 7
        - As there is a sacred Scripture, a sacred book, and a sacred Person, so there is also divine arithmetic.
        - Because these seven churches have spiritual characteristics that Christ finds in His churches throughout the centuries, these seven are chosen out of a multitude of others in Asia.
        - In speaking to these seven churches, Christ was speaking to all churches.
     b. Urgency and immediacy
        - The second reason for these churches to represent all of the churches of Christ is because of the urgency and immediacy with which these letters are composed and addressed.
        - Each time the letters are addressed to a church, they are based upon the authentication of the Lord God Himself.
        - For example, to the church at Ephesus: *"These things saith he that…"* (2:1) is followed by an attribute of the Lord.
        - Notice all seven of the introductions.
     c. The conclusions
        - The third reason is the letters' conclusions—all of them alike: *"He that hath an ear, let him hear what the Spirit saith unto the churches"* (Revelation 2:7, 11, 17, 29; 3:6, 13, 22).
     d. Mysteries
        - The seven churches and seven pastors are called mysteries.
        - Therefore, there is some mysterious thing Christ is going to reveal about them.
     e. The book of prophecy
        - There is something significant about the letters to these seven churches because the messages are found in this book of prophecy.
        - Right here at the heart of this prophecy, these chapters are dedicated to the seven churches of Asia.

4. The Seven Periods in the History of the Church, as Compared to the Seven Churches
   - The seven churches provides the entire story of the church through all of the centuries. They are a panoramic view of the history of the churches. The seven churches represent historical periods in the history of the people of Christ.
   a. The Ephesian period
      - A period that witnessed the cooling of love and devotion, such as the church at the conclusion of the days of the apostles.
      - There was a waning and a lessening, a dissipation of the first love.
   b. The Smyrnian period
      - To the church at Smyrna, Christ had no word of condemnation.
      - It is the only one of the seven letters that is entirely made up of praise and encouragement.
      - This is the church of martyrdom and catacombs.
   c. The Pergamian period
      - Christ says, in effect, "You are now seated where Satan's throne is." (See Revelation 2:13.) In other words, the church is married to the world.
      - In history, Constantine performed the ceremony.
      - The church at Pergamos was introduced to the doctrine of the Nicolaitans, which is the exaltation of the clergy.
   d. The Thyatirian period
      - In the development of Christianity, this is the rebellion of the church.
      - This is the era of the scarlet woman.
      - It is the church committing spiritual adultery with the nations of the earth.
      - It is the Papal church, which denied grace for works.
      - It is the false teaching, casting out love and abiding evil.
   e. The Sardian period
      - The Sardian church is the church of the great reformation.
      - There are *a few names even in Sardis which have not defiled their garments*" (3:4).
      - This Sardian period in our church history is known as the Reformation.
   f. The Philadelphian period
      - The era of the open door.
      - It is the far-flung missionary endeavor, because the Lord says, "*I have set before thee an open door*" (3:8).
   g. The Laodicean period
      - When the church says, "*I am rich and increased with goods, and have need of nothing*" (3:17), the Lord replies, "[You] *knowest not that thou are wretched, and miserable, and poor, and blind, and naked*" (verse 17).
      - The Laodicean church is the church of the final stage of apostasy.
      - It is the period of ease and complacency—a period of *doing* rather than *being*, which marks our present age.
5. Coexistence
   - As we look at these churches, the fact that all of them coexist through history, in every age, country, and denomination is an amazing thing. There are Ephesian churches that cool off and lose their

first love, Smyrnian churches that are oppressed and their people martyred, Laodicean churches in which people could care less about the gospel but only think of their own social needs.

- The seven churches also coexist within almost every church. For example, in practically every church you will find lackadaisical Ephesian members, Smyrnian members who pay for their devotion with grief and tears, Laodicean members who prefer the social affairs more than the difficult work of God, and so on.

- The burning message that Jesus had for us today can be found in Revelation 2:29. Look up this verse.

_____

_____

_____

6. The Seven Parts of the Seven Letters
   - All of the seven letters to the seven churches of Asia are designed alike. They all follow a distinct pattern. Here is the format for each of the letters:
   a. The salutation
      - This tells us to whom the letter is sent, such as: *"Unto the angel of the church of Ephesus… in Smyrna… in Pergamos…,"* etc. All seven letters begin with those identical words.
   b. Attributes of the Lord Jesus
      - The second part presents a description of the Lord.
      - All of these attributes are found in John's vision of the Lord Jesus in Revelation 1.
      - An example would be: *"These things saith he that holdeth the seven stars in his right hand"* (2:1)—the same attribute found in Revelation 1:16.
      - In the second church, Smyrna, you find the words, *"These things saith the first and the last, which was dead, and is alive"* (2:8). This is found in Revelation 1:17–18.
   c. Works of the church
      - All seven letters have a statement concerning the works of the church.
      - In each one, Christ says, *"I know thy works…."*
   d. What Christ sees
      - The fourth part of each letter contains Christ's characterization of each church and what He sees them doing.
      - He describes what they are and what they are not doing.
      - He praises them in some cases, and condemns them in others.
   e. The second coming
      - The fifth part of each letter always makes reference to Christ's second coming.
      - He describes how His coming will appear to each church.
   f. Universal admonition
      - The sixth part of each letter is a universal admonition to hear.
      - *"He that hath an ear, let him hear what the Spirit saith unto the churches."*
   g. A final promise
      - The seventh part of each letter is a final promise.
      - For instance, in the first church, Ephesus, you read: *"To him that overcometh will I give to eat of the tree of life"* (2:7), etc.

♦ In the last four letters, the sixth and seventh parts are switched. The promise is placed as the sixth part and the admonition is seventh. We don't know why. But the distinct thing to remember is that all the letters have the same seven characteristics and follow the same pattern. The area of rewards for the seven churches is a complete lesson within themselves, but I will try to just add them briefly as we go through the seven churches in the upcoming lessons.

## How Much Do You Remember?

1. The second section in the structure of the book of Revelation includes chapters 2 and 3. What do these chapters address?

2. What do the seven churches represent and what are the five reasons that prove this?

3. Look back if needed and name the seven periods of the church's history.

   _____, _____, _____,

   _____, _____, _____,

   _____.

4. How many parts make up each letter to the seven churches?

5. What are the parts to each letter and what difference can be found in the last four letters?

## Your Assignment for Next Week:

1. Revisit chapter 2 of Revelation. Look for the outline of each letter as presented in this lesson.

2. Review your notes from this lesson.

3. Underline your Bible.

## Lesson 3 Notes

_____

_____

_____

_____

_____

_____

_____

_____

_____

_____

_____

_____

_____

_____

_____

_____

_____

# Lesson 4
# REVELATION 2

## The Letter to the Church at Ephesus (Revelation 2:1–7)

1. The City of Ephesus
   - Ephesus was, at that time, a large city with an excellent harbor. It was a marketplace for all of Asia.
   - Ephesus was an important religious city.
   - The temple of Diana—Artemis, as the Greeks called her—was considered one of the seven wonders of the ancient world.
   - The banking center of that vast metropolis was in a vault in the temple of Diana.
   - The goddess Diana was the patron of all the prostitutes. Her image stood everywhere.
   - You will recall the story of Acts 19:13–19, in which graven images of Diana were made by the silversmiths in the city of Ephesus.
   - Black magic was also widely practiced in Ephesus.
   - Paul met these occult people head on and led some of them to Christ.
   - The Christian church at Ephesus was extremely well taught, having had Paul, then Apollos, then Timothy, and then John as pastors.

2. The Letter
   a. The salutation
      - *"Unto the angel of the church of Ephesus write…"*
   b. Attributes of the Lord Jesus
      - Christ describes Himself here as the one who *"holdeth the seven stars* [messengers] *in his right hand"* (2:1). Each church messenger was protected and held accountable for faithfully conveying God's message.
   c. Works of the church
      - In the words of commendation about the church at Ephesus, you will find seven things the Lord Jesus had to say about the church:
        1.) First, *"I know thy works"* (2:2).
           - It was an active, energetic church. They were in business for the Lord.
           - It was a church that worked and it was a church that made an impression upon all of the city.
        2.) Second, the Lord commends them for *"thy labor"* (2:2).
           - This meant they worked, they toiled at a cost.
           - The task was not something incidental to them. They not only worked for God, but their work had a cost. Their paid the price for their faith.
           - Many love to eat of the clusters of the vineyard, but few like to toil in the cultivation of that vineyard. The people at Ephesus were pouring their lives, souls, and hearts into that church, and they meant business for God.
        3.) A third thing the Lord commends this church for is *"thy patience"* (2:2).
           - This means they had a triumphant attitude.

- No matter how much the Ephesian Christians were beaten down or discouraged or persecuted, they did not quit.

4.) A fourth thing the Lord Jesus says about Ephesus is *"and how thou canst not bear them which are evil"* (2:2).

- Christ noticed that they were sensitive to the presence of evil. They did not become accustomed to it so that they did not notice it.

5.) The fifth thing for which Christ comments this church is this: *"Thou hast tried them which say they are apostles, and are not, and hast found them liars"* (2:2).

- Doctrinally, the believers at Ephesus were very competent in their stand against false teaching. This is evident by their expulsion of the false prophets.

- There were those who came there claiming to be apostles of Jesus Christ, but the people at Ephesus tried them and found to be liars.

- In the church at Ephesus, when a man showed himself to be a doubter and questioner of the faith, they could not stand him.

6.) The sixth thing he commends this church for is *"and [you] hast borne"* (2:3).

- Do you notice the things they cannot bear? They cannot bear evil and they cannot bear false doctrine and doubts—but they *can* bear toil, sacrifice, and persecution.

7.) The seventh thing he commends the church for is this: *"and hast patience, and for my name's sake hast laboured, and hast not fainted"* (2:3).

- In other words, they are people who stick with it, at any cost. They don't faint and they don't fail.

- The heart of the real Christian is this: that he or she is willing, in God's hands, to be God's servant, as God shall choose. And they do not faint.

d. Praise and admonition

- After He names the seven attributes of the church at Ephesus, He does have a complaint about them, which He characterizes in verse 2:4. Look up this criticism for the church at Ephesus:

_____

_____

_____

- Despite all of the good things Christ had to say about the church at Ephesus—they had *"left [their] first love."*

- We can see examples of this in the present-day church and in individuals. The old, abounding joy and gladness of being a Christian seems to slip away and service toward the Lord becomes mechanical, ritualistic, and routine.

- The Lord speaks to this church, saying, *"Remember therefore from whence thou art fallen, and repent, and do the first works"* (2:5).

- These people are to remember and to repent. They forget how many times the Lord has helped them, and how Christ has met every need in their lives. So, Christ says to the Ephesians, *"Remember...."* Then He urges them to *"repent"* of their loveless Christian duty and to get off of their routine of works and return instead to the love for Him they originally had when they first walked in the wonder and excitement of salvation.

e. Second coming
- Notice that Christ mentions His coming when He says, *"Or else I will come unto thee quickly"* (2:5).

f. Universal admonition
- Christ admonishes the church, saying, *"He that hath an ear, let him hear what the Spirit saith unto the churches"* (2:7).
- This is a universal admonition written to each of the seven churches.

g. Final promise
- Christ concludes His words to the church at Ephesus when He says, *"to him that overcometh will I give to eat of the tree of life, which is in the midst of the paradise of God"* (2:7).
- This is the promise of the Lord to the church of Ephesus and to us.
- To the one who listens and overcomes, Jesus promises that he will eat of the tree of life in God's everlasting paradise.
- An overcomer is one who believes in Jesus as the Son of God and has received Him as Savior and Lord. (See 1 John 5:4–5.)
- The tree of life is referred to again in Revelation chapter 21.

The Ephesian church is a prophetic picture of the apostolic church. Like the church of Ephesus, the dominant, historical characteristics of the apostolic church were correct conduct and labor for the Lord. As their love for Christ began to decline, they more and more served out a sense of duty. They made up in *doing* what they lacked in *being*.

## The Letter to the Church at Smyrna (Revelation 2:8–11)

1. The City of Smyrna
- Smyrna was the great port city that derived its name from the fragrance and perfume of Myrrh.
- Myrrh, or Smyrna, is a type of suffering. Myrrh was used to embalm the dead and it typifies the suffering of our Lord for our sins.
- The very name of this city, and the church in that city, brings to mind tribulation and persecution. This is the church of great trial and tribulation.
- The city of Smyrna is one of the truly great ancient cities of the world. As far back as history goes, there was a city located in Smyrna.
- Today it is, by far, the largest metropolis in Asia Minor. It has a population of more than four million people and is presently known as Izmir, the Turkish word for Smyrna.
- Even today, most of the seven locations of these seven churches are nothing but ruins, but Smyrna, or Izmir, lives on as one of the leading cities of that part of the world.
- Smyrna was one of the most proud cities of all of Asia. It was proud of being a most beautiful city, and more especially, of being the center of Caesar worship in the eastern part of the Roman Empire.
- To the city of Smyrna, worldly things were *"the first and the last"* (2:8). God was not supreme. To Smyrna, the first and the last were the glories of Greek culture and the magnificence of their beautiful city.
- The life of the people of Smyrna was organized around cultural programs and athletic contests held in a great arena that held twenty thousand people (smaller than the one at Ephesus). They also celebrated festival days and worshiped in beautiful temples.

2. The Church of Smyrna
- The church at Smyrna was different from the city of Smyrna.

- The church in Smyrna suffered tribulation and persecution. There are three reasons why this bitter persecution was the daily lot in life of the poor, humble church.
  a. First, the Christian church there stood on the site of a continuous and spectacular display of paganism.
    - The little church was meager as compared to the marvelous Greek temples.
    - Had the people been willing to take their Savior and put Him alongside Apollo, Aphrodite, Hermes, and any of the other thousand pagan deities, they would have been received with all gladness. But that was one thing the Christians would not do.
    - Remember that the economic and social life of the Greek cities was organized around the cults. Every man who worked belonged to some kind of guild, which we would call an organization or union—and every guild had a certain patron god or goddess. Days of festivals and worship were set aside for these guilds. When the Christians refused to participate in this activity, they were immediately marked for retribution.
    - The Christian in Smyrna stood particularly alone, and his faith cut him off from the job that would help him exist and provide a living for his family. His faith in Christ set him apart as being strange and peculiar. In Smyrna, it was terribly different to be a Christian.
  b. Second was the fact that Smyrna was the great center of Caesar worship.
    - This is one of the keys to the understanding of the book of Revelation. The background of all of the Revelation is set against the cult of emperor worship.
    - The Roman Empire covered the known civilized world at the time of John's writing. The one thing that united the Roman Empire was the Roman spirit, and that spirit is what made the Roman Empire Rome.
  c. Third was the heavy hand upon the Christian by the state itself.
    - To be a Christian anywhere in the empire was to take one's life into his own hands, but this was especially true in the city of Smyrna.
3. The Letter to the Church at Smyrna
  a. Salutation
    - Look up the salutation to the church at Smyrna, found in the first half Revelation 2:8:

    _____

  b. Attributes of the Lord Jesus
    - Look up the attribute of Jesus given after the salutation in the second half of Revelation 2:8:

    _____

  c. Works of the church
    1.) *"I know thy works"* (2:9).
      - This contains the idea of pressure that forces the blood, or the pressure of persecution and sorrow and even death.
    2.) *"I know thy poverty, but thou art rich"* (2:9).
      - That word *"poverty"* actually means "utter destitution." The Christians at Smyrna were destitute despite living in one of the richest cities in all the Roman Empire.
      - They were poorer due to the fact that they were deprived of the right to work because they served the Lord Jesus and would not bow down to Roman worship.

- Therefore, they were severely persecuted and lived in utter want. They did not have jobs because they would not join a guild. They did not have homes; they had to beg for bread and were completely destitute.

3.) *"I know the blasphemy of them which say they are Jews, and are not, but are the synagogue of Satan"* (2:9).

- Here, the word *"blasphemy"* means slander. There were false Jews in Smyrna who slandered the Christians.

- One of the most famous martyrdoms in all history happened in this city. The pastor and leader of the Christians in this city was Polycarp. He was brought before the Roman governor and given the choice of professing Caesar or Jesus as lord. Polycarp's answer to the governor was simple: "Fourscore and six years have I served Him, and He has never done me injury; how then can I blaspheme my King and Savior?" As he was burned, Polycarp prayed, "I thank Thee that Thou hast graciously thought me worthy of this day and of this hour, that I may receive a portion in the number of Thy martyrs."

d. Praise and admonition

- Look at the words of encouragement to the church at Smyrna in verse 10: *"Fear none of these things which thou shalt suffer: behold, the devil shall cast some of you into prison, that ye may be tried; and ye shall have tribulation ten days: be thou faithful unto death, and I will give thee a crown of life."*

- So the Lord knows about the tribulation, the works, and the poverty of those people, and He assures them of something better, because He, Christ, had experienced it all. Thus, He says, *"I know."*

- The Lord states firmly, *"Fear none of these things which thou shalt suffer...and ye shall have tribulation ten days."* Some refer to these ten days as being the ten prophetic eras of persecution under ten Caesars, and it could well be, but I think the Lord means simply this: the number ten is an intensive number. Forty is four intensified. Seventy is seven intensified. The word *"ten"* refers to a fierce and intense persecution, like the ten plagues in the land of Egypt.

- They were to *"fear none of these things"* and, rather, to be *"faithful unto death."* Then they would receive *"a crown of life."* This is the reward for the suffering or martyred Christian. Those ten days actually coincide in history with the persecution of ten Caesars, and they start with Nero in A.D. 64 and cease with Diocletian in 312.

e. Universal admonition

- Look up the admonition to hear in the first part of Revelation 2:11.

_____

_____

_____

f. Final promise

- Look up the final promise given in the second part of Revelation 2:11.

_____

_____

_____

## The Letter to the Church at Pergamos (Revelation 2:12–17)

Pergamos is the church that compromises with the world system. It was a letter sent to the angel, messenger, or the pastor of the church at Pergamos.

1. The City of Pergamos
   + Pergamos was a blend of political power, pagan worship, and academic sophistication.
   + It was at one time the capital city of Asia Minor and royal officials filled it with beautiful palaces and temples.
   + It was one of the influential learning centers, with a great university and a library of more than two hundred thousand books, second only to the library in Alexandria, Egypt.
   + The Pergamene god was the god of healing, and its emblem was a serpent. Pergamos became a great city for healing.
   + In the courts of the temple, snakes crawled on the ground as the afflicted came from the ends of the earth to sleep in the sanctuary. They believed that healing was possible in the presence of their healing god if the sick happened to be touched by one of those slithering snakes.
   + Much of what the people of Pergamos called medicine we could call unadulterated superstition.
   + The city of Pergamos was a famous shrine and effectively drew the sick from all ends of the empire.
   + From this city, and from this background of the serpent healing, came the caduceus—the medical symbol of a short staff entwined by two serpents.

2. The Letter
   a. The salutation
      + *"And to the angel of the church in Pergamos write…"* (2:12).
   b. Attributes of Jesus
      + The description of Christ is given as having a *"sharp sword with two edges"* (2:12), similar to the attributes mentioned in Revelation 1:16.
      + Observe the difference when Christ addresses the Pergamene church. Here is a God of love and mercy, but He is also the God of justice, righteousness, and judgment. To this church, He says, *"So hast thou also them that hold the doctrine of the Nicolaitanes which thing I hate."*
   c. Works of the church
      + Look up where Jesus addresses the works of the church as Pergamos in Revelation 2:13:

   _____

   _____

   _____

   _____

   _____

      + The Lord praises these saints for continuing to boldly proclaim Him as the only Lord, even in the face of great danger and opposition.
      + Many Christians died for their faith, but Jesus singles out one: Antipas. He calls him *"my faithful martyr"* (2:13). He was just an obscure man in history who was totally committed to Christ, however, he is the one we remember when we think of ancient Pergamos. It is believed that Antipas was the first martyr put to death by the Roman Empire. He was never mentioned afterward nor was he mentioned before.

- Notice: *"I know thy works and where thou dwellest, even where Satan's seat is."* Here, the Lord is telling them, "I know where you are, and I know your circumstances, and even though you are in the midst of satanic conditions, I know you are there."

d. Praise and admonition

    1.) The Lord commends the church for these things:

- He commends the church for being faithful in verse 13: *"and thou holdest fast my name."* The church stood for the name of Christ, even in the face of danger and opposition.
- The Lord commends the church when He says *"and hast not denied my faith."*

    2.) The Lord has these things against the church:

- The Lord had this grievance against the church there: *"thou hast there them that hold the doctrine of Balaam, who taught Balac to cast a stumblingblock before the children of Israel, to eat things sacrificed unto idols, and to commit fornication"* (2:14).
- The doctrine of Balaam is the teaching and the council of a shrewd character. He could not curse Israel. God would not let him, as you will read in Numbers 31:15–16, but he did something worse to corrupt God's people—he introduced them to strange Moabite women. The Moabite women corrupted Israel, a thing that Balaam himself could not do.
- The Lord spoke to the church in Pergamos and told them to beware, because through this sensual activity, the doctrine of Balaam would cast a stumbling block in front of them, like Balaam did before the children of Israel.
- The Lord also refers to *"things sacrificed unto idols."* When the ancient worshipper made a sacrifice to an idol, such as Zeus, the animal was not burned. Only a few of its hairs were tossed into the fire. The priest and the worshipper would then divide the sacrificed animal meat. Had these false teachers succeeded in convincing Christians that it was proper to eat not only the meat offered unto false idols, but also the holy bread of the Lord's Supper, Christianity would have been swamped and would have died in the seas of paganism. The true Christians in Pergamos said, "I will not drink and I will not eat."
- *"So hast thou also them that hold the doctrine of the Nicolaitanes, which thing I hate."* What is this teaching of Nicolaitans (modern spelling)? There are two areas of this doctrine:

    a.) The name

- The word *"Nicolaitanes"* is composed of two simple Greek words—*nike*, meaning victory, and *laity*, which is derived from the Greek word *laos*, meaning people. Together, this word refers to a group or class of people who exalt themselves above others.

    b.) The Pergamene period of the church

- This is the church of the establishment. It is the day when the church is married to the world.
- Look at the name *Pergamos*. *Per*, referring to something objectionable, and *gamos*, the word for marriage. This word *gamos* also helps to form the words *polygamy* or *bigamy*.

- The Pergamene period of the church is the period of the marriage of the world to the church. But it is a perverted marriage, therefore, you have Pergamos.
- Put all these meanings together and we shall have a good idea of what the doctrine of the Nicolaitans is all about. *Nico-laos*, the conquerors, the victors, the subjugators of the people; *Pergamos*, the Pergamene period of the church when it is exalted and married to the very household of the Roman Empire.
- The doctrine is this: The rising up of a class of people, apart from and exalted over a great mass of God's people. This class granted themselves power above the people: the power of life and death, the power to forgive sins, the power to excommunicate, and the power to damn others to hell. They alone had the power to interpret and to mediate the Word and the will of God. Their doctrine is the subjugation of the people. Their leaders enter into the political, military, and governmental arenas of the world. What had become a sporadic seed thought in Ephesus, has become now a strong, dynamic doctrine.
- The doctrine of Nicolaitans is the doctrine of sacramental salvation. According to that doctrine, one is converted not by the power of the Spirit of God but by the sacrament of christening a baby into the membership of a church.

e. Second coming
  - *"Repent; or else I will come unto thee quickly, and will fight against them with the sword of my mouth* [the Word of God]*"* (2:16).
  - This message is still true today, and the church needs to repent and return quickly to the Word of God.

f. Admonition to hear
  - *"He that hath an ear, let him hear"* (2:17).

g. Final promise
  - *"To him that overcometh will I give to eat of the hidden manna, and will give him a white stone, and in the stone a new name written, which no man knoweth saving he that receiveth it"* (2:17).
  - Manna was one of the things placed in the ark of the covenant and was one of the things provided by the Lord God to the children of Israel. When manna came down from heaven, it was gathered, placed in a golden bowl, and placed in the ark before the Lord, hidden behind the veil. This is why the Lord says, *"I give to eat of the hidden manna."*
  - There are many strange interpretations as to the meaning of the white stone referenced in this final promise. Some say it is a little white ball, used when you don't want to vote against someone (if you want to black ball them you use a black ball.) Others think this white stone refers to those little charms with mystic names on them, worn in order to keep people safe and away from disease and death. I think *"a white stone"* means a beautiful, crystal-clear gem—a diamond. The urim of the breastplate of the priest was a diamond, and those who sought to know God's would look at it, on which was written the mystic name of God.

## The Letter to the Church at Thyatira (Revelation 2:18–29)
1. Background
   - The fruits of evil are now being reaped as we now see in the church at Thyatira.
   - In Ephesus, the believers lost their first love and became occupied with other things.

- In Smyrna, the doctrine of true grace had been diluted with legalism until the synagogue of Satan was making its way into the midst of the church.

- In Pergamos, we have seen the church married to the world and the doctrines of Balaam. The Nicolaitans were exalted and low levels of conduct became common.

- The next church is the papal church. As we study it, we shall see many changes taking place in this particular church.

- The central theme of this letter is God's judgment upon Jezebel. She calls her works "the deep things of God," but God calls them "the deep things of Satan."

2. The Letter

   a. The salutation

- *"And unto the angel of the church in Thyatira write"* (2:18).

   b. Attributes of our Lord Jesus

- Notice how the Lord introduces Himself as *"the Son of God"* (2:18). He uses this strong language because of a prophetess who calls herself Jezebel, and who denies the Word of God and proclaims that she is infallible. Therefore, the Lord says, "I am the Son of God."

- Then He adds, *"Who hath his eyes like unto a flame of fire, and his feet like fine brass"* (2:18).

- His eyes can penetrate into the deepest recesses of the heart. He comes as a judge and walks among the church at Thyatira.

- The quotation *"his feet are like fine brass"* is a statement of judgment. It indicates the fierceness and the wrath of God.

   c. Works of the church

- Look up the works of this church in verse 19 of this chapter:

_____

_____

_____

- Increased works are the badge and the credential of a believer.

- Works always follow faith, it is not the other way around. The same applies to a seed; the seed has to be planted first, then there grows a genuine product. So it is with faith; you have faith—specifically, surrendering faith in Christ—and then works are produced.

- *"Thy last works"* (2:19). To those faithful few who were remnant in the church at Thyatira, the last works were more—they had increased rather than diminished in those who were truly believers.

   d. What Christ sees

- In verse 20, the Lord says, *"I have a few things against thee,"* and then He mentions the adulterous situation in Thyatira.

- This woman is referred to by the Lord as Jezebel.

- Her name takes us back to Israel. Ahab, the king, married the daughter of the king of Sidon, whose name was Jezebel. (See 1 Kings 16:31.) When she came to live in the capital city of Samaria, she brought her heathen gods with her and introduced Israel to idolatry. She then leads Israel into its worst days of apostasy.

- But who is this Jezebel of Thyatira who claims to be a prophetess? Some claim she is the wife of the pastor at the church of Thyatira. Others think she was a prophetess in the famous oracle, called Sambathe.

- We know Jezebel's identification because it is plain. The book is a book of prophecy and God is speaking here of a development in the church in the age of the Thyatiran history of His people. The church is always represented by a woman, as "she, and as the "bride of Christ." So, in this passage, when we see a woman, we see a figure of the church; and when that woman is called Jezebel, we immediately note that the Lord is speaking of an apostate church.

- Notice in verse 21 that the Lord says, "*I gave her space* [or time] *to repent of her fornication; and she repented not.*" Historically, He gave this church about a thousand years to repent—from about A.D. 500 to 1500.

- There is not a record anywhere of any church or organization that has reformed and repented. Any gigantic movement for Christ in the past has come from God-called individuals who were in the church, but shook the world without a denomination backing them. There is a limit to which false doctrine and false teaching can go, and so, God Himself shall take care of that, as He does here at Thyatira.

- In verses 22–23, He says, "*I will cast her into a bed, and them that commit adultery with her into great tribulation, except they repent of their deeds. And I will kill her children with death.*" This judgment is described at length in Revelation 17. God will not put up forever with Jezebel and the seduction of His people.

- "*And all the churches shall know that I am he which searcheth the reins and hearts: and I will give unto every one of you according to your works*" (2:23). The word "*reins*" means kidneys or viscera. Notice, the Lord mentions nothing about the head, but only the inward man, the inside.

e. Second coming
- "*Hold fast till I come*" (2:25).
- The Lord is telling them, "Hold on. Don't give up. Don't quit. I will not give you more than you can bear."
- The morning star from verse 28 is also the announcement of the dawn. If we have Christ, and remain in Him, then we have been caught away with Him and shall appear with Him when He appears in glory.

f. Universal Admonition
- "*He that hath an ear, let him hear what the Spirit saith unto the churches*" (2:29). What a period—what a message for our day.
- He is going to take the church, the remnant, out of our world before its hour of tribulation.
- This is why the Savior came, choosing and cleansing the church, and presenting it to Himself glorified, without spot or wrinkle. This is the fulfillment of the great mystery of the spiritual marriage between Christ and the church, as described in Ephesians 5:22–32.

g. Final promise
- But the Lord has a word of hope for Thyatira.
- In verses 24–25: "*I will put upon you none other burden. But that which ye have already hold fast till I come.*"
- God has a second reward to the faithful in verse 28: "*And I will give him the morning star.*" In Revelation 22:16, the Lord describes Himself as "*the bright and morning star.*" When Christ gives us the morning star—we have Him.

## How Much Do You Remember?

1. Which four letters are included in chapter 2 of Revelation?
2. What was God's complaint toward the church of Ephesus?
3. What does the name Smyrna, or Myrrh, mean? How does this meaning correlate to the happenings of the church at Smyrna, and what were the three reasons for this?
4. What two doctrines does God admonish the Pergamene people for exalting?
5. Who or what is the Lord referring to when He spoke of Jezebel in the letter to Thyatira? What is Jezebel's identity?
6. What is the meaning of the morning star written in the letter to Thyatira, in reference to the Lord's second coming and His promise to the people there?

## Your Assignment for Next Week

1. Revisit Revelation 3 and look for the outline of each letter as presented in lesson 3.
2. Review your notes from this lesson.
3. Underline your Bible.

## Lesson 4 Notes

_____

_____

_____

_____

_____

_____

_____

_____

_____

_____

_____

_____

_____

_____

_____

_____

_____

_____

_____

# Lesson 5
# REVELATION 3

## The Letter to the Church at Sardis (Revelation 3:1–6)

1. A Correlation to Parables

   ♦ There is a distinct break between the messages spoken to the first four churches in chapter 2 and those messages that now follow.

   ♦ The whole character of these last three letters—that is, to the churches at Sardis, Philadelphia, and Laodicea—differs greatly from the first four.

   ♦ This can be brought out in a striking fashion by a comparison with the parables of Matthew 13.

   ♦ You will recall that the Lord had been busy on the Sabbath morning when these parables were spoken. He had been criticized by the Pharisees because his disciples had picked grain on the Sabbath. Jesus took the occasion to give another great message on the relationships between Himself and those who were doing the Father's will. The houses in the villages emptied and crows followed Him. From a boat, He these great parables that prophesied the outward characteristics of Christendom. We shall see how the first four of these parables correspond to the first four letters to the churches of Asia.

   ♦ When the Lord had completed the parable of the leaven (Thyatira), He rose from His place in the boat and dismissed the crowd and went into a house as His disciples followed. Therefore, it can readily be seen that the first four parables are what we might call "outside" parables. The last three may be called "inside" parables.

      a. Ephesus had been the church of the wheat sown on good ground, bringing forth fruit, but the first love had been lost.

      b. By the time of Smyrna, the tares had taken root, and within the boundaries of the visible church were those whom the risen Lord saw as the synagogue of Satan.

      c. By the time the Pergamos stage was reached, the third of the parables was finding its fulfillment—the mustard seed, which the Lord meant to be nothing more than an herb grown into a large tree. The birds of the air—the devil's birds—came to lodge in its branches.

      d. The fourth is the parable of a woman who hid leaven in a meal, as we saw depicted by the character Jezebel as we studied the church at Thyatira.

      e. Finally, at the church in Sardis in the fifth parable, we find that the treasure is hidden in a field. When a man finds it, he hides it. So it is with this church in Sardis, when we read in Revelation 3 that "they had a name to live and were dead." (See Revelation 3:1.)

2. The Church at Sardis

   ♦ Sardis can be described as a church that had the form, but its heart was gone.

   ♦ Christ was theirs in word, but ignored in deed—their creeds were correct and their conduct respectable, but spiritual life had departed.

   ♦ It was a place in which ritual was practiced, but Christ was forgotten.

   ♦ Sardis is only about thirty miles from Thyatira, and about sixty miles southeast from Pergamos.

3. The Letter

   a. Salutation

      ♦ *"And unto the angel of the church in Sardis write…"* (Revelation 3:1).

b. Attributes of the Lord Jesus
- You will find the Lord introducing Himself as *"he that hath the seven Spirits of God, and the seven stars"* (3:1).
- We already know that the seven Spirits of God refer to the complete work of the Holy Spirit. Here, Christ reasserts that the Lord Jesus wishes to control His church by the effective work of the Holy Spirit. It is the total Spirit, as described in Isaiah 11.
- He also has the seven stars in His hands—the seven messengers or pastors. You will note that He has them in His hand. He always protects those who are faithful to the teaching and preaching of His Word, and here, He holds them in His hand.

c. Works of the church
- *"I know thy works, that thou hast a name that thou livest, and art dead. Be watchful, and strengthen the things which remain, that are ready to die: for I have not found thy works perfect before God"* (3:1–2).

d. What Christ sees
- In verse 3, He says to *"remember therefore how thou hast received and heard, and hold fast, and repent."*
- The manner of hearing is always the same—it is by the work of the Holy Spirit.
- In Romans 10:17, we read, *"Faith cometh by hearing, and hearing by the word of God."*
- Sardis had received the Word. During the days of Sardis, they had all of the gospel and they were to observe the things that they had received and heard.
- There are only a few words of commendation in verse 4: *"Thou hast a few names even in Sardis which have not defiled their garments; and they walk with me in white: for they are worthy."*
- The emphasis upon names in this particular message should be noted. The church had a name to live, but it was dead. There were only a few names that defiled not their garments.

e. Second coming
- There is a warning here to those who will not watch. The Lord says in verse 3, *"I will come on thee as a thief, and thou shalt not know what hour."*
- Here, His coming refers to the Second Advent.
- The first phase of this coming is as a bridegroom, and the second phase is as a thief, to take the church out unto Himself.
- The heart of this message to Sardis is that those who trust in the fact that their names are written in some church roll or book are dead. If they refuse to leave this dead, spiritual life, and if they refuse to promote Christ above the tradition of the church—they have missed the Lord's coming as a bridegroom, but they will remain for His coming as a thief in the night.

f. Universal admonition
- Once more, the message concludes with the definite word to the individual in verse 6: *"He that hath an ear hear. Let him hear what the Spirit saith unto the churches."*

g. Final promise
- Now to them, the believers, *"they shall walk with me in white: for they are worthy"* (3:4).
- Throughout Scripture, righteousness is synonymous with this symbol of white garments.
- Notice that the overcomer will not have his or her name blotted out of the Book of Life, but that Christ shall confess their names before the Father.

- This promise needs no comment because it speaks for itself. It is the same as you will find in Luke 12:8, which says, *"Whosoever shall confess me before men, him shall the Son of man also confess before the angels of God."*

## The Letter to the Church at Philadelphia (Revelation 3:7–13)

1. The Philadelphian Period
   - We are shown the pathway into another period, which we call the Philadelphian period—or the church of the open door.
   - So, from Thyatira, when Satan seemingly has full control, to the message at Sardis, where only a few held fast to the Word of God, next we see the message to the church at Philadelphia—the new era of preaching, teaching, and spreading the Word of the Lord Jesus.
   - Philadelphia means "brotherly love." Philadelphia was to manifest love. John expressed it in his epistle in 1 John 4:7–8, which says, *"Beloved, let us love one another: for love is of God; and every one that loveth is born of God, and knoweth God. He that loveth not knoweth not God; for God is love."*
   - The Philadelphia-type church is still present in the world, and it will be here until the rapture, but it is not the dominant force in the professing Christianity of today.

2. The City of Philadelphia
   - The city of Philadelphia was founded about 140 B.C. by the king of Pergamos, whose name was Philadelphus. The city was named after him.
   - Philadelphia was located where three great countries joined together—the ancient lands of Mysia, Lydia, and Phrygia.
   - It was for this purpose that the city was founded on that particular site, in order that it might spread Greek language, culture, literature, and manners to the world.
   - An unusual thing that reflected what the people of Philadelphia knew is reflected in Revelation 3:12: *"And he shall go no more out."* What does this mean? Philadelphia was located before a vast volcanic field and was subject to severe earthquakes. Many times, the city would be devastated by the tremors of the earthquakes. When they came, people fled for fear. But here, Christ speaks of the perpetual, everlasting, eternal security that we have in Him, and so, He used language common in that day to teach a spiritual lesson to those people—and to us.
   - The city of Philadelphia is located about twenty-eight miles southeast of Sardis and is, even to this day, largely a Christian town.

3. The Church of Philadelphia
   - The church at Philadelphia is the church of the open door.
   - Throughout Scripture, the Lord reflects the history and the geographical situations when He speaks and teaches. For instance, one thing the Lord says to this church is, *"Behold, I have set before thee an open door"* (3:8).
   - The Lord had nothing but words of commendation for Smyrna, the martyr church—and He has almost nothing but words of commendation for this missionary church of Philadelphia.
   - The Philadelphian church is the church of our closing era. It is the church of missionaries, evangelists, and Bible societies.
   - It is the church of the worldwide preaching of the gospel of the Son of God.
   - This church represents the missionary movement. It also represents the revived church in that day.
   - The Philadelphian church or period extends to the present hour, and since Philadelphia means "brotherly love" and "the church of the open door," it suggests that we must begin with our own

witnessing at the front steps of our own church and homes, down the street and across the street, out into the community, into the states, and around the world.

4. The Letter

   a. The salutation

         + *"And to the angel* [messenger or pastor] *of the church in Philadelphia write..."* (3:7)

   b. Attributes of the Lord Jesus

       1.) *"These things saith he that is holy, he that is true, he that hath the key of David"* (3:7).

            + Here, the Lord introduces Himself as one who is holy. He is the Holy One because He was conceived of the Holy Spirit and He lived a life that was holy. (See John 10:36–37.)

            + He also introduces Himself as *"he that is true."* In John 1:9, He is called *"the true light, which lighteth every man that cometh into the world."* In John 14:6, He says, *"I am the way, the truth, and the life."* In John 15:1, He says, *"I am the true vine."*

            + So we see that Christ is holy and that He is true in every respect.

       2.) Then He says, *"He that hath the key of David, he that openeth, and no man shutteth; and shutteth, and no man openeth"* (Revelation 3:7).

            + This can also be found in Isaiah 22:22. Look up this verse to compare:

_____

_____

_____

_____

            + In Isaiah, we find a characterization of Eliakim, the steward of King Hezekiah. This trusted man was given the key to the palace. No one came to approach the king except through Eliakim. So it is with us in Christ. There is an open door to God in our Savior, and no man can shut it.

            + The door to prayer and intercession is always open.

            + When Jesus says that He possesses the key of David, it is a reminder to the Jews in Philadelphia that the Davidic covenant, which promised eternal blessing through David's greater Son, Christ, shall and will be fulfilled in Jesus Himself.

   c. Works of the church

       1.) *"I know thy works"* (3:8).

            + Works are always a result of faith.

            + The works mentioned here are in reference to an open door.

            + Jesus said, in so many words, "because of your works, I will set before you an open door."

            + We have seen that door gradually close within the last few decades, but the Lord will not allow the door to be shut as long as we stay by Him and keep His Word.

       2.) We read in verse 8: *"For thou hast a little strength, and hast kept my word, and hast not denied my name."*

            + This means they were not a strong church, not an influential church. Yet, even though they are not strong, the Lord promised to keep that door open because they still had faith, kept His Word, and had not denied His name.

- The last part of verse 8 is meaningful: *"thou hast not denied my name."* In other words, stay true to the Word of God, true to the things that are taught in this book. Do not deny the Word of any part of it. Stay true to the virgin birth, the deity of Christ, the bodily resurrection, and all the essential elements that we claim as a basis for our faith.

d.  What Christ sees
   1.) In verse 9, the Lord says, *"Behold, I will make them of the synagogue of Satan, which say they are Jews, and are not, but do lie; behold, I will make them come and worship before thy feet, and to know that I have loved thee."*
      - Jesus says, in effect, "As for those who are considered a part of the synagogue of Satan, who say they are Jews even though they are not, I will make them come and worship, respect, or bow down before you who are Christians."
      - Why does He say this? Notice the last line of verse 9: *"to know that I have loved thee."* We too should copy this love of Christ, and it is called brotherly love, which means Philadelphia, which is the key to this church.
   2.) *"Because thou hast kept the word of my patience, I also will keep thee from the hour of temptation, which shall come upon all the world, to try them that dwell upon the earth"* (3:10).
      - We must take this verse literally. He shall remain up from the hour of tribulation.
      - What is the *"word of my patience"*? I think it refers to us patiently waiting for Christ. In 2 Thessalonians 3:5, Paul says, *"The Lord direct your hearts into the love of God, and into the patient waiting for Christ."*
      - *"I also will keep thee from"*—the test referred to as *"the hour of temptation"* is a test for the earth-dwellers, not for believers. We cannot be judged with the world because the Bible says we are passed from death into life. The next thing on our calendar of activities, and on the calendar of God, is the rapture of the church.

e.  Second coming
   - *"Behold, I come quickly: hold that fast which thou hast, that no man take thy crown"* (3:11).
   - Two things here are of utmost importance to us:
      1.) First, He is going to come quickly and shall take His pearl of great price—the church. This promise of His coming again is something that helps us to keep living the Christian life.
      2.) Second, He says, *"Hold that fast which thou hast, that no man take thy crown."* In other words, hold on to what you have, because that will be your reward.
   - There are two things I want you to remember about what the Lord has given to us:
      1.) First, heaven and salvation is no reward. *They are gifts of the Lord Jesus Christ.*
      2.) Second, rewards (or crowns) are given for works *after* salvation. We are given the gifts to work for Him, but rewards are given by the Lord Jesus for the things that we do for His name and His glory after we have been saved.
   - He is to come quickly, and none of us who claim the name of Christ shall go through the hour of tribulation.

f.  Universal admonition
   - In this letter, the admonition to hear is the closing of the letter.
   - *"He that hath an ear, let him hear what the Spirit saith unto the churches"* (3:13).

- We must hear through the Holy Spirit interpreting the Word of God for us.

   g.   Final promise

      1.)  *"Him that overcometh will I make a pillar in the temple of my God"* (3:12).

- In heaven, there is no moveable temple. John says that in the New Jerusalem, he saw no temple, for the Lord God and the Lamb are the temple.

- When he says we are to be a pillar in the temple of God. He is saying that, in heaven, God's people have an eternity with God Himself.

- What is a pillar? It is for strength, adornment, beauty, and commemoration. God has chosen us in the eternity of eternities to be the witness of, the adornment to, and the commemoration of His grace, love, and mercy.

- In the New Jerusalem, we are the adornment and the expression of all that God is—love, mercy, grace, beauty, and holiness—world without end.

      2.)  *"And he shall go no more out"* (3:12).

- We are to be pillars and shall go no more out.

- In the courses of the priests, death took them out of their ministry. Even our first parents were driven out, beyond Eden, to sweat and to work the sod.

- But in the New Jerusalem, we shall not ever have to go out of the city of God anymore.

      3.)  *"And I will write upon him the name of my God, and the name of the city of my God, which is new Jerusalem, which cometh down out of heaven from my God: and I will write upon him my new name"* (3:12).

- Like the high priest of old, we shall have all the dignity of that high office, carrying with it the right of access to God forever.

- Notice these words, *"Wherefore God also hath highly exalted him, and given him a name which is above every name: that at the name of Jesus every knee should bow, of things in heaven, and things in earth, and things under the earth"* (Philippians 2:9–11).

- He never lays aside His old names, but there are also achievements, victories, and triumphs of which man can never completely comprehend, and of which we have heard or dreamed to be accorded to our Lord Jesus Christ.

# The Letter to the Church at Laodicea (Revelation 3:14–22)

1.  The City of Laodicea

- This is the last letter to the churches of Asia. It is written to the believers at Laodicea.

- Laodicea is the most southeasterly church in Turkey.

- The name Laodicea is rich in meaning. It was founded by Antiochus II, who named the city after his wife, Laodicea.

- About fifteen miles east of this church you will find the ancient city of Colossae.

- Laodicea means "justice of the people."

- In this city, there was great wealth, science, and literature. It was the center of industry.

- In building the city, Jews were offered free citizenship to entice them to live in the new city. The reason for this was that the Jews brought trade with them, and trade meant wealth, commerce, banking, and manufacturing. This was especially true of Laodicea.

- Laodicean wealth came in no small part from the garment industry of the city. The Lord uses the common customs of the day to teach spiritual truths, admonishing these people to *"buy...white raiment, that thou mayest be clothed"* (3:18).

- There was a medical center in Laodicea. One of the products manufactured and exported, among other medical products, was a small tablet that was crushed and put on the eyes of all of those who had an eye ailment. People all over the Roman empire bought these tablets. The Lord refers us to this when He says, *"anoint thine eyes with eyesalve, that thou mayest see"* (3:18).

2. The Church at Laodicea

- Laodicea is an interesting city and an interesting church, but most of all, it is meaningful to us because it represents the last of the churches.

- What will the churches be like when the Lord comes again? The church at Laodicea represents the last period in church history. The Laodicean church is the church of the end time. This fact makes every syllable of this particular passage of Scripture important.

- Out of all the churches written by the Spirit of God, there is only one church for which the Lord had nothing to say in the way of commendation and encouragement—the church at Laodicea.

- The Laodicean church is described as a lukewarm church, neither cold nor hot. It was indifferent to doctrine, truth, and the teaching of God. To the Laodiceans, one church was about as good as another.

- Laodicea departed in practice from the truths of God—but its position before God is unquestionable and the Lord makes that very clear.

3. The Letter

 a. Salutation

- *"Unto the angel of the church of the Laodiceans write..."* (3:14).

- You will note that the church is recognized and is called by name.

- The spiritual condition of this assembly, even in Paul's day, thirty years prior, caused the apostle great mental conflict, as you can read in Colossians 2:1.

 b. Attributes of the Lord Jesus

  1.) *"These things saith the Amen..."* (3:14).

- The word *"Amen"* is used as a proper name for Christ. The word signifies that which is fixed, that which is true, and that which is unchangeable.

- In Greek, it would be translated in our well known usage of the word *verily*. This name has a note of finality to it. This indicates that Christ has the final word.

- In His person, we have the guarantee that every promise and every truth will be "amened."

  2.) *"The faithful and true witness..."* (3:14).

- Christ is the one who reveals all and tells all. We should never look to a man or a church, but to the *"faithful and true witness."*

- He tells this church at Laodicea that He is the faithful and true witness because the church there was a wreck. The most responsible witness that Christ has ever had on the earth is the church, but in this Laodicean period, the church is being morally ruined not by open enemies but by professed do-gooders—believers who are boastful and proud, wealthy and content with Christ on the outside, but cold and indifferent in their inner lives.

  3.) *"The beginning of the creation of God..."* (3:14).

- Christ now speaks of Himself as Creator. Paul also states this emphatically in Colossians 1:15–19.
- He is the Creator and He is the Consummator.
- This very fact intimates the ruin of creation—of which the church is the last witness.
- He is the one who is the Beginning because He is the one who holds all things together.

c. Works of the church
- *"I know thy works, that thou art neither cold nor hot: I would thou wert cold or hot"* (3:15).
- Laodicea is representative of the age in which we live. It is described as being rich and having all the worldly adornments, yet they were neither cold nor hot.
- The terms used are *"cold"* and *"hot"*—not *"dead"* and *"alive."*
- Had these last two descriptions been used, the truth of being saved or lost might have been in question, but begin *"neither cold nor hot"* is used to describe their relation to Christ.
- Total indifference to Christ, not hatred, is implied in the term *"lukewarm"* (3:16).
- There is nothing worse than having a neutral, uncommitted position toward Christ. Because of this, the Lord tells them what He will do.

d. What Christ sees
1.) *"So then because thou art lukewarm, and neither cold nor hot, I will spew thee out of my mouth"* (3:16).
- Lukewarmness makes the Lord sick. The church—or the organization called the church—is spewed out and not a part of the rapture.
- There is an organization called "the church" that will go through the tribulation. It will have all the outward appearance of a rich and comfortable church, but it will not be a part of the body of Christ.
- Remember that the true and false may enter the house, but only the true can enter the Body. So the Lord says to those who are false, *"I will spew thee out of my mouth."*
- Remember that Philadelphia is cheered with a promise of *"I come quickly"*; Laodicea is threatened with judgment: *"I will spew thee out of my mouth."*
- The repudiation of the Lord from this church will come about by the translation of the saints. In other words, the removal of all true believers and the rejection of the worldly Laodicean attitude.

2.) *"Because thou sayest, I am rich, and increased with goods, and have need of nothing; and knowest not that thou art wretched, and miserable, and poor, and blind, and naked"* (3:17).
- In verse 17, we read the Lord's condemnation. Remember that Philadelphia had not a word to say for itself, but Laodicea has.
- Notice the Lord says, *"thou sayest."* Not only was there a self-satisfied condition in this church, there was also a proud boasting mentioned by the Lord when He says, *"Thou sayest, I am rich."*
- Without doubt, this church had influence, numbers, gifts, intellectual acquirements, and other attractive qualities—and it prided itself in all of them. That these things existed at the expense of spirituality, and at the expense of a fervent

love for Christ, can only be regarded as a curse, and must, if not repented, end in judgment.

- ✦ They could boast while immediate judgment was announced in verse 16, and Christ, who should be the church's life and glory, was standing outside as we shall see in verse 20.
- ✦ How does the Lord look upon all of this? He says, *"Thou art the wretched, and miserable, and poor, and blind, and naked"* (3:17).
- ✦ They were poor because they had no real riches, only money. There were blind to their own state, and to the Lord's glory, and naked of all divine righteousness.
- ✦ *"And knowest not..."* (3:17). Their own actual condition before the Lord was completely unknown to those people.
- ✦ Do you see a parallel in our day? I do not know of a more common attitude in the world today than the one of "I" and the attitude of humanism.

3.) *"I counsel thee to buy of me gold tried in the fire, that thou mayest be rich; and white raiment, that thou mayest be clothed, and that the shame of thy nakedness do not appear; and anoint thine eyes with eyesalve, that thou mayest see"* (3:18).

- ✦ We find in this verse three main characteristics of Laodicea: poverty, nakedness, and blindness. And the Lord offers them grace.
- ✦ The Lord is gentle here. He could have commanded them to do certain things, but instead, He councils them: *"Buy of me gold purified by fire"* (3:18). Gold, purified or refined by fire, points to divine righteousness, which is tested and tried. Without it, how poor we become.
- ✦ The term *"white raiment"* is declared because it represents the righteousness of those who believe in the Lord. These white garments would cover their moral nakedness and the shame of their life.
- ✦ *"Eyesalve"* I believe to be the Holy Spirit, and it is to be applied to the eyes for spiritual discernment so they can see the true and spiritual things.

4.) *"As many as I love, I rebuke and chasten: be zealous therefore, and repent"* (3:19).

- ✦ Throughout the wording to this church, the Lord has been speaking in tones of unusual severity. The circumstances call for it. But for Christians, then and now, they were to know that the Lord's rebuke and chastening are the fruit of His love.
- ✦ In other words, He would rekindle their interest. This is the first step toward recovery for that church, and for us.

e. Second coming
- ✦ There is no mention of the second coming in the letter to the church at Laodicea.

f. Universal admonition
- ✦ *"He that hath an ear, let him hear what the Spirit saith unto the churches"* (3:22).
- ✦ This verse concludes the letter to the Laodiceans and the third chapter of Revelation.
- ✦ It is the duty of the *individual* to hear.

g. Final promise
- ✦ Now we come to one of the most precious verses in all of Revelation. This touching and tender call has, for centuries, been the foundation of many Christian songs and sermons.

  1.) *"Behold, I stand at the door..."* (3:20).

- This is spoken to individuals only, unlike other verses that were addressed to the collective body.
- Notice here that the Lord takes an outside place. He is morally disowning the professing church.
- The Lord both speaks and knocks, and what a rich display of grace this is in the worst of circumstances.
- The Lord neither commands nor does He force entrance.

2.) *"If any man hear my voice, and open the door, I will come in unto him, and sup with him, and he with me"* (3:20).
- This means the last meal of the day, the last activity before the dawn of a new day.
- Remember, this is for individuals. The text indicates that He continues to stand and knock because He wants the place in the hearts of his own.

3.) *"To him that overcometh will I grant to sit with me in my throne, even as I also overcame, and am set down with my Father in his throne"* (3:21).
- This is one of the most striking of all the things said by the Lord Jesus to His churches.
- The letters, like this one to Laodicea, are addressed to congregations, ministers, and churches, but always the appeal is to the individual heart and to the individual soul.
- The Lord, as He speaks to His congregations, rebukes and counsels, exhorts and indicates judgment. But when He makes an appeal, it is always addressed in the singular, to the individual.
- The promise of our Lord to the believing soul is found in this verse. The throne is the sign and symbol of royal authority and dominion.
- The Lord Jesus is in that exalted position because of His life of patience and His death for us and for the glory of God.
- The reward to the overcomer is a glorious one. You will remember that an overcomer is described in 1 John 5:4–5. Look up this Scripture in the King James Version for a better understanding of the term *overcomer*:

_____

_____

_____

_____

_____

_____

- The Laodicean conqueror—the person who lives in this age but is true to the Word of God and his faith in Christ—is promised a part of the riches of Christ, in His kingdom and glory.
- Surely a rich and full reward in overcoming the Laodicean element is spoken of in this passage.

Now we have finished the study of the seven churches. The lessons in church history contained in chapters two and three of Revelation are invaluable. To have heaven's wording and light thrown on the conditions during this church period of almost two thousand years is a mercy that is second to none.

## How Much Do You Remember?

1. Which letters are contained in this chapter of Revelation?
2. What was the attitude toward Christ of the church at Sardis?
3. How does the Lord tell the church at Sardis about how He will come again, and what is His promise to the believers there?
4. What was the church at Philadelphia referred to as?
5. What is God's promise to the overcomers in Philadelphia?
6. Which church is only one that received no words of commendation from the Lord?
7. What attributes does the Lord use to describe Himself to the Laodiceans?
8. What is the attitude of the Laodiceans toward Christ?
9. Review verse 18 and recall what the terms *"tried in the fire,"* *"white raiment,"* and *"eyesalve"* symbolize.
10. What was God's promise to the Laodiceans?

## Your Assignment for Next Week:

1. Read Revelation 4.
2. Review your notes from this lesson.
3. Underline your Bible.

## Lesson 5 Notes

_____

_____

_____

_____

_____

_____

_____

_____

_____

_____

_____

_____

_____

_____

_____

_____

_____

# Lesson 6
# REVELATION 4

*"Write...the things which shall be hereafter"* (Revelation 1:19).

1. The Third Great Part

   - In chapter 4, we come to the third and final great section of the Revelation, as it is outlined by the Spirit of God.

   - Thus, God divided the book of Revelation into three great parts and He commanded John to write down those three great parts in Revelation 1:19. We have studied two of them.

   - First: *"Write the things which thou hast seen."*

   - Second: *"Write…the things which are."* And those things are, of course, the churches, addressed in chapters 2 and 3.

   - Then the third part: *"Write…the things which shall be hereafter."* The meaning is "write the things that shall be when the churches are no more; write the things that shall be after the churches."

   - When we come, therefore, to Revelation 4, we are entering the final consummation of the age. All church history now is past. The thousands of years that God has been using His ministers and the Word to uphold the light of Christ in His churches are no more—they are taken away.

   - Beginning in chapter 4, we enter the great period of the judgment of God upon the earth—after God's people are taken away.

2. The Disappearance of the Churches

   - This is an astonishing thing. The churches disappear in chapter 4.

   - Heretofore, the churches have occupied the central place as God views history, but at the end of chapter 3 and beginning with chapter 4, the churches disappear. There are no more churches; they are not mentioned.

   - Some think they are referred to under the name of Israel—but I ask in return, do the churches have twelve tribes and are they divided according to the tribe of Judah, the tribe of Simeon, the tribe of Reuben, and so forth?

   - The next time we see the church is in Revelation 19 at the end of the age. She is there, the bride of Christ, coming with her Lord in glory.

   - How did she get there? She disappears at the first verse in chapter 4, and the next time we see the church is in chapter 19. So I ask, how did she get up there with the Lord? That is what Paul calls, in Greek, a *musterion*, or a mystery.

   - To us, a mystery is an enigma, a riddle, something devious and hard to find out. But in the Bible, a *musterion* (a mystery) is a secret in the heart of God, which a man can never learn by himself; God has to reveal it. (See, for instance, Romans 16:25; Ephesians 3:3–5, 8-10.)

3. The Old English Word *Rapture*

   - The word *rapture* is an old English word built upon the Latin word *rapare*, or *raptum*. It means to transport, to take away, or to snatch away.

   - *Rapture* in the modern English language has come to mean "ecstasy," because when a man is transported out of his senses, he is beyond himself. We say that he is "enraptured" or swept off his feet. We have come to apply the word to the way we feel.

- But we should remember that the basic teaching and meaning of the word *rapture* is "to take away." So when we speak of the rapture of the church, we are speaking of taking away the people of God— the calling up or the transporting to glory all of the household of faith.

- This, too, Paul says is a mystery—something that God has revealed to His churches—in Acts 7:55–56.

4  A Door Opened in Heaven—Revelation 4:1

- Every word of this verse is meaningful: *"After this I looked, and, behold, a door was opened in heaven: and the first voice which I heard was as it were of a trumpet talking with me; which said, Come up hither, and I will shew thee things which must be hereafter."*

- This verse is a type and a picture of the door of the ascension of God's sainted people.

- That trumpet voice is the type and symbol of the voice of the archangel of God, sounding like a trumpet that raises the dead from their graves, and that, according to the word of our Savior, gathers His elect from the four winds of the earth. That is the great trumpet voice that summons to heaven God's sainted children in the earth.

- Notice the words especially, *"Come up hither, and I will shew thee things which must be hereafter."* That is the type and the picture of God's children rising to be with their Lord in glory.

- Then, after the door is opened in heaven, and after the great call of God to His sainted dead and those of us who are living who are saved—in other words, after the rapture of the church—the Holy Spirit writes, "I will show you things that must be the things that are after these things."

- At the end of the Philadelphian age, the door is beginning to close. In the Laodicean age, the door is closed and Christ is knocking on the outside. But when the door begins to close at the end of the Philadelphian age and the Laodicean Period seems to be rampant around the world, that is the signal for the door of heaven to open. When it is opened, God says to the apostle John, *"a door was opened…come up hither."* Just as ambassadors are called home before war is declared, so it is for us. Before these things can happen to the world, God must first remove all who belong to Him, for the fire and judgment cannot fall until we *"come hither."*

- The rest of the book of Revelation is a description of that awful and terrible period when God has taken His people out of the earth and when He pours upon this world the judgments of the wrath of the Almighty.

- Beginning with chapter 4, and on to the consummation, we have the revelation, the unveiling of the end time of the world, the great and terrible days of the tribulation.

5.  The Deliverance of God's People

- In Isaiah 13, Joel 1–2, and 2 Thessalonians 2:2, the time is called *"the day of the Lord"* or *"the day of Christ."*

- In Jeremiah 30:7, the time is called *"the time of Jacob's trouble."*

- In Daniel 12, that time is described as being *"a time of trouble, such as never was since there was a nation even to that time"* (Daniel 12:1). It is a day of awesome terror.

- This day is the outbreak and the outpouring of the judgments of the almighty God on iniquity and sin, and on those who reject the overtures of grace—when God shall say "enough." It will be the day of the *great tribulation.*

- Where will we be? Where will our people, God's people, the church, the saints, God's redeemed ones be during this terrible tribulation? Will those who believe go through the tribulation? Every answer of Scripture is, emphatically, *no.*

- As long as believers are on this earth, those judgments cannot fall. As long as God's people are present, those horrible and terrible things that shall take place in the tribulation will never come to pass.

6. God's Churches and the Great Tribulation

+ We shall see now why the churches of the Lord Jesus will not go through this terrible period of trial and tribulation.

+ There are four reasons why God's people will not go through the terrible time of trial and trouble:

a. Structural background and outline of the book of Revelation itself

+ Recorded in Revelation 1:19.

+ How had the church come to be in heaven? She was taken up, raptured, which was a mystery revealed to us in Scripture.

+ In Revelation, a door was opened in heaven and a voice as a trumpet was heard saying, *"Come up hither"*—vividly portraying the calling away of the people of Christ, of whom John is a representative. Thus, God's people are not to be judged.

+ You will find that described in 2 Corinthians 5:10, when we shall all stand at the judgment seat of Christ. That is the judgment of *rewards*.

+ Romans 8:1 says, *"There is therefore now no condemnation to them which are in Christ Jesus."* In Revelation 3:10, the Lord says, *"Because thou hast kept the word of my patience, I also will keep thee from the hour of temptation, which shall come upon all the world."*

b. 2 Thessalonians 2:2–3

+ The second reason as to why God's people shall not pass through the terrible tribulation is found in this Scripture.

+ The Christians in Thessalonica were in great trial. They thought they were in the days of the tribulation and they asked Paul what was happening.

+ Paul explained this to them in 2 Thessalonians 2:3. Look up this verse:

_____

_____

_____

+ Some texts interpret this as God's people being raptured away, but Paul continues with the explanation that the first thing that shall happen in that awful day of the Lord and the judgment of God upon this earth is to be the revelation of the man of sin.

+ There is a restrainer in this earth, the Holy Spirit of God, and He is in His people. Someday the Holy Spirit of God in His churches and in His people will be taken away, and after that happens, the man of sin will be revealed and be the one to usher in the Great Tribulation.

c. Types and illustrations used to describe those awful times

+ In Luke 17:26, 28, 30, the Lord says, *"And as it was in the days of Noe, so shall it be also in the days of the coming of the Son of man…. Likewise also as it was in the days of Lot…. Even thus shall it be in the day when the Son of man is revealed."*

+ Take this one example and look at the fact that in the days of Noah, in the days of the judgment of God upon the earth, in the days of the flood, Enoch was taken out before the flood, Noah sailed over the flood, and the vile, wicked, unbelieving world perished in the floor.

+ Enoch is a type and a picture of God's people, who are taken out before the tribulation.

- Lot was a carnal, compromising Christian, but the angel said to Lot, *"I cannot do anything till thou be come thither"* (Genesis 19:22). As long as Lot was in Sodom, the fire could not fall, the brimstone could not burn, and the judgment could not come.
- Before that judgment falls, and before the awesome days of the Great Tribulation, God's people must be taken away, for God will not let that judgment fall until first the restraining Spirit—the people of God—are taken away.

d.  Scriptural presentation of the comfort and the hope of the Christian
- While some look for the man of sin, the beast or false prophet, or the tribulation and trials, God's people are told to look only for the blessed Holy Savior. We are to look for Him.
- As Paul wrote in Titus 2:13: *"Looking for that blessed hope, and the glorious appearing of the great God and our Saviour Jesus Christ."*
- It is false to put anything between the promise of the eminent, immediate return of Christ and its actual fulfillment. The coming of Christ is always at hand. We are to live with the eminent return of Christ in our mind.
- He will come silently, quietly, and come for the pearl of great price, which He has purchased with His own blood. He is coming for His jewels, which happens to be the church.

7.  John's First Insight into Heaven (verses 2 and 3)
- The door that has been opened in heaven has now enabled the church—and John in his vision—to pass into heaven.

a.  The throne
- What John sees is almost indescribable, but you will notice that, immediately, he saw the throne there in heaven. Throughout the rest of Revelation, the throne of God is the central object of all that takes place.
- Its stability is conveyed in the word *"set."* It is fixed definitely and precisely and it becomes a seat of royal authority. The thrones of this world do not last, but the throne in heaven is our security and strength.
- The *"one"* upon the throne is unnamed but is described in various significant terms. Two precious stones are named, and what John saw was like those stones—*"like a jasper and a sardine stone"* (4:3). We would call those diamonds and rubies. By these stones, the glory and majesty of God are reflected.
- His essential glory cannot, of course, be communicated—and it was not communicated here to John. But John did see all that the Bible ever indicates one sees of God, because God is spirit. This is reflected in 1 Timothy 6:16.  Look up this verse:

_____

_____

_____

_____

b.  The rainbow
- Notice also that John sees a rainbow around the throne, *"in sight like unto an emerald"* (4:3).
- This great throne in heaven, encircled by a rainbow, is a witness that almighty God will graciously remember His people in covenant mercy.
- The purpose of that rainbow can be found in Genesis 9:11–17. In that covenant, God promised that the world would never again be completely destroyed by water, and He also

proclaimed that as long as the present earth existed, the four seasons would continue and that there would be light and darkness as well as sun and heat.

- This rainbow around God's throne is a gracious reminder that God will remember His promise of mercy, even during the awful days of tribulation.

- The reference of an emerald is significant because it is green in color instead of the combination of colors that we are accustomed to seeing in a rainbow. This one is a beautiful green; the characteristic color that God uses all over the universe. It is the color of the plant world and the only one that never tires the eye.

- The glorified saints—all of us who are part of the body of Christ—will have constantly before our eyes the rainbow in its entirety; the remembrance of God's grace to the earth, even when He is about to deal in judgment with those on earth.

8. The Four and Twenty Elders (Revelation 4:4)

   a.  Who they are not

- Who are the twenty-four elders? They are not spirits. It is beyond our thinking and certainly foreign to the revelation of God that spirits should be clothed, crowned, or even seated.

- These twenty four elders are not angels. In the description of these who give praise to God, they are always separated and delineated from angels. Examples of this can be found in Revelation 5:11.

   b.  Who they are

- The twenty-four are God's saints—His redeemed, His blood-bought people. They are enthroned in heaven, seated around the great central throne of God.

- They number twenty-four, twice twelve, represent the twelve patriarchs of Israel and the twelve apostles of the Lamb. Together they make up God's redeemed society. This is the same system of numbers you will find in John's description of the beautiful city, the New Jerusalem. There are twelve gates, and on those gates are the names of the twelve tribes of Israel. On the twelve foundations are written the names of the twelve apostles of the Lamb. The twelve of Israel and the twelve of the church make up the twenty-four elders, seated before the throne.

- Notice these four and twenty elders are clothed in white raiment and have crowns of gold on their heads. Both of these things are true about born again believers. The white robe always symbolizes righteousness and the crowns are rewards given by the Lord Jesus.

9. Verse 5: *"And out of the throne proceeded lightnings and thunderings and voices: and there were seven lamps of fire burning before the throne, which are the seven Spirits of God."*

- You will notice that the words *"out of"* and not *"from"* proceed *"lightnings and thunderings and voices."* This is an indication that God is getting ready to begin judgment. Lightning and thunder proceeding out of the throne means a storm—a serious storm.

- You will also note that there were seven lamps of fire burning before the throne, which are the seven Spirits of God. In chapter 1, we saw these same seven lamps on earth, with Christ walking among them. Now these lamps are in heaven, further evidence that God will remove the church prior to the Tribulation period.

- Also in chapter 1, we were introduced to the seven Spirits of God and saw that this symbolized the seven characteristics of the Holy Spirit, as indicated in Isaiah 11:2. This further proves that the church will be removed, because the seven lamps are before the throne and they are the seven Spirits of God.

10. *"And before the throne there was a sea of glass like unto crystal"* (4:6).

- The word *"sea"* in biblical terms always symbolizes the restless masses of people.

- The word is used in this way in Revelation 13 and several times in the book of Isaiah. Isaiah compares the nations with the troubled sea. This is amazing because in Revelation 15:2, we will find *"a sea of glass mingled with fire,"* expressive of the ordeal that shall be going on at that time.

- But here before the throne, the sea is like glass, motionless. This pictures the believers at rest in the presence of God. There is no more storm—it is calm, quiet, and peaceful.

11.  The Four Living Beasts (verses 6–11)

*And round about the throne, were four beasts [in Greek, zoa, or "living things"] full of eyes before and behind. And the first beast [zo-on, or "living one"] was like a lion, and the second beast like a calf [like an ox], and the third beast had a face as a man, and the fourth beast was like a flying eagle. And the four beasts [zoa] had each of them six wings about him; and they were full of eyes within: and they rest not day and night, saying, Holy, holy, holy, L*ord* God Almighty, which was, and is, and is to come. And when those beasts give glory and honour and thanks to him that sat on the throne, who liveth for ever and ever, the four and twenty elders fall down before him that sat on the throne, and worship him that liveth for ever and ever, and cast their crowns before the throne, saying, Thou art worthy, O Lord, to receive glory and honor and power: for thou hast created all things, and for thy pleasure they are and were created.*

- We are going to talk about these four living creatures that you find throughout the Old Testament, beginning in the third chapter of Genesis in the building of the tabernacle.

- You will find them in the Ezekiel 10, and they are usually referred to as the four cherubim of God.

  a.  What is the meaning of the four living ones in the book of Revelation?

      1.) They have to do with the world.

      - They have to do with God's purposes in this created life.

      - They are four in number, which means the world.

      - There are four seasons, four points to the compass, four elements, and four winds. Four is the number that refers to the earth.

      - The Jew of the Talmud said that there were four who were primary among the forms of life that God made: first among all created life, man; second among all domestic life, the ox; third among all untamed life, the lion; and fourth among the bird of heaven, the flying eagle. These are the four faces of the cherubim. They have to do with God's created life in this world.

      2.) The cherubim have to do with the implementation and the execution of God's purposes and decrees for this world and for the life He has created.

      - Their assignment is the execution of the decrees and purposes of God in human history.

      - In this chapter, we read, *"out of the throne proceeded lightnings and thunderings and voices."* We know, therefore, that the throne here is a throne of judgment.

      - The truth is plainly assigned and delineated to the cherubim in the Revelation. We see this openly revealed as we begin in chapter 6 in a subsequent lesson, when we find the Lamb opening the seals and one of those four cherubim says, "Come." And then comes a white horse—the anti-Christ, a false prophet of peace, conquering and ready to conquer. Continuing in that chapter, you will find that all four of the cherubim, the *zoa*, the living ones, play a part.

3.) The cherubim are emblems, instruments, and insignia of the love and purposes of the grace for us and for God's creation.

- In the garden of Eden, when the man and the woman were driven out, cherubim (living ones) were placed at the gate on the east side, to guard the tree of life, lest the man, in his sin and his mortality, eat thereof and live forever.

4.) They signify the protective care in our earthly life.

- The old rabbis, in commenting on the second chapter of Numbers, said that the twelve tribes of the children of Israel, in marching three times on each side of the encampment, marches under four banners, four standards, four ensigns of the administrative and judicial purposes of God.
- The standard of Judah was the lion, and on that side, three tribes gathered.
- The standard of Reuben was a man, and on that side, three tribes gathered.
- The standard of Dan was a flying eagle, and on that side, three tribes gathered.
- The standard of Ephraim was an ox, and on that side, three tribes gathered.
- The twelve tribes gathered round the central glory of God, marching through the wilderness under the banner of a lion, an ox, a man, and an eagle, and you see that exactly in Revelation 4:7.
- So the four *zoa*, the four living ones, are emblems of God's protective care.

5.) The four living ones speak of the attributes of God.

- They are described as "*full of eyes before and behind,*" which gives us an idea of the fullness of spiritual intelligence.
- They can see what has happened in the past and they can see what shall happen in the future.
- As four is the number of man and of creation, we see that these four living ones are associated with God's governmental and judicial dealings.

6.) They compare with the four presentations of our blessed Lord.

- Matthew reveals Him as the Lion of the tribe of Judah.
- Mark describes Him as the Servant—the ox.
- Luke describes Him as the Son of Man, His identification with man.
- John reveals Him as the Son of God, the eagle. He comes from heaven and returns from whence He came.

b. How do the Cherubim worship?

- In verses 9–11, we find that as these four living creatures cry the triune holiness of the Lord God seated upon the central throne that "*the four and twenty elders fall down before him…and worship him that liveth for ever and ever.*" (4:10)
- This is the song of redemption. This fourth chapter ends with a song of praise.
- When those four cherubim give glory, honor, and thanks, the four and twenty elders fall down to worship also. Thus, now there is one who is worthy to receive praise from all of creation, because we see in verse 11 the reason for our being when we read the words, "*for thou hast created all things, and for thy pleasure they are and were created.*"

## How Much Do You Remember?

1. What happens to the churches in the beginning of chapter 4?
2. Describe the significance of the verse: *"Behold, a door was opened in heaven…. Come up hither."* What does this mean for the believers in the time of judgment?
3. What are the four reasons that support why God's people will not go through the tribulation?
4. What is the first and central thing John sees in his insight into heaven? What does this central thing represent for us?
5. What is the rainbow surrounding the throne a reminder of?
6. Who are the twenty-four elders?
7. Describe the faces of the four beasts and some of the many symbolic connections that can be made to them.
8. How does chapter four conclude?

## Your Assignment for Next Week:

1. Read chapter five of Revelation.
2. Review your notes from this lesson.
3. Underline your Bible.

## Lesson 6 Notes

_____

_____

_____

_____

_____

_____

_____

_____

_____

_____

_____

_____

_____

_____

_____

_____

_____

_____

# Lesson 7
# REVELATION 5

Chapters 4 and 5 in the book of Revelation go together. There is a chapter division for our convenience, but it should not be allowed to destroy the continuity of the record that John wrote. Chapters 4 and 5 record the scenes that John saw with his own eyes when he looked upon glory. The scene, as it develops, brings into focus an all-important scroll that is laid upon the hand of God.

1. The Book Sealed with Seven Seals

    a. What John sees

    - In verse 1, you will notice that the scroll is *"in the right hand of him that sat on the throne."* That book, or scroll, was sealed with seven seals.

    - Remember, when we use the term *"book,"* we refer to the book as it was in the ancient day. The scroll was the only kind of a book known when the Bible was written.

    - This scroll that lay in the hand of God was sealed with seven seals. It was really sealed— literally, *"sealed with seven seals."*

    - Now the vision that John saw was this—there was a scroll rolled up, then part sealed, then rolled again, and sealed, rolled again, and sealed, etc.—through all six seals. Then the seventh seal sealed the entire scroll. When it was unsealed, the process was reversed. When the first seal was broken, a portion of the scroll could be unrolled and read. When the second seal was broken, another portion of the scroll was unbound and read, and so on, until all seven seals were broken and the entire scroll was opened.

    - There is great significance in that book. As we proceed through the book of Revelation, we shall see that this is one of the most vital and significant of all the scenes that we are to look upon, as they are depicted on the apocalypse.

    b. The meaning of the scroll

    - There are many theories about the meaning of this scroll, but here are four points that I think it represents:

        1.) First, it brings into the heavenly scene the Son of God, the Prince of glory, and the Redeemer of creation, which is the beginning of those final events leading to a new heaven and a new earth.

        2.) Second, it introduces us to the Lamb of God. The Prince of glory, who takes it, does so in the character of the Lamb, slain on the sacrificial altar, a Lamb with its blood poured out upon the earth. The character of the One who comes, the great matchless Son of God, is the character of the Redeemer, the sacrificial Lamb.

        3.) Third, when that One comes to take that book, He comes in a character and in a work from whom all creation has shied away because of their unworthiness and inability.

        4.) Fourth, when the scroll is taken by the hand of Him who is the great Redeemer of the world, all creation will burst into song.

    - Therefore, it is my understanding that the primary, fundamental, and chief reference and significance to this book has to do with the redemption of God's created universe and everything in it. That book is a book of redemption. It is a book of the final acts of God concerning the things that are yet to come. It is a book of judgment; it is a book of the last days and of casting Satan, the dragon, into hell; and it is the overcoming of the grave, death, and sin.

- Seven is the number of perfection. Therefore, this scroll contains the perfect will and purpose of God in regard to this world. Before these purposes could be revealed, the seals had to be broken. Hence, a strong angel proclaimed with a loud voice, *"Who is worthy to open the book, and to loose the seals thereof?"* (5:2)

- Verse 3 tells us that *"no man in heaven, nor in earth, neither under the earth, was able to open the book, neither to look thereon."*

2. *"I wept much"*

- In verse 4, John says, *"I wept much."* This represents the tears of all of God's people through all the centuries.

- This verse, I think, is put in here because it describes the heartache of all of the redeemed of the Lord and of the ones who have been in such a position as John. It shows the tenderness and longing for the great Redeemer, and, as John writes, *"I wept much, because no man was found worthy"* (5:4).

- Then, in verse 5, one of the elders says, *"Weep not."* Notice, it is one of the elders—one of the redeemed, one of the blood bought. *"One of the elders saith unto me, Weep not behold...."*

- That has been the cry of the church through all the centuries—weep not, lift up your heads, lift up your hearts, look, behold, wait, the Lamb of God, the Savior of the world is on His way.

3. The Lion of the Tribe of Judah

- One of the elders said to John, *"Weep not, behold, the Lion of the tribe of Judah, the Root of David, hath prevailed to open the book, and to loose the seven seals thereof"* (5:5).

- The phrase *"the Lion of the tribe of Judah"* is familiar and we know what that refers to.

- In Genesis 49:8–10, when Israel was prophesying of his twelve songs, he turned to the fourth boy, Judah, and said,

  *Judah, thou art he whom thy brethren shall praise: they hand shall be in the neck of thine enemies; thy father's children shall bow down before thee. Judah is a lion's whelp: from the prey, my son, thou art gone up: he stooped down, he crouched as a lion, and as an old lion; who shall rouse him up? The scepter shall not depart from Judah, nor a lawgiver from between his feet, until Shiloh come; and unto him shall the gathering of the people be.*

- Notice the words, *"until Shiloh come."* In His Lion-like character, He crushes every opposing force and establishes His universal kingdom.

- In Isaiah 11:10, Romans 15:12, and Revelation 22:16, we find reference to the Root and offspring of David. Why David and not Moses, Abraham, or Elijah? David is chosen because he was preeminently the king, and that king represents God's purpose for His Son in the earth.

- He shall reign over the whole creation. The sovereignty of the earth and the authority of all creation are in His hands, the Root of David, the offspring of David.

- Abraham is of promise, Moses is of the law, Elijah is of the prophets, but David is of the kings. The kingdom is of the Lord's. It belongs to the Lion of the tribe of Judah, the Root and the offspring of David. He was the only one who could prevail to open the book and loose the seven seals.

4. The Lamb

- Now, in verse 6, notice: *"In the midst of the four and twenty elders, **stood** a **Lamb** as it had been slain."*

- He saw a lamb. That same word is used twice in the New Testament. Once it is used in John 21:15, where the Lord asked Peter if he loved Him and Peter said, "You know I do." Then the Lord said, *"Take care of My little lambs."* The other time it is used is here in the book of Revelation.

- Here, in the midst of the four living creatures, the four and twenty elders, and God's redeemed saints, John saw a Lamb. The lamb was violently slain. The signs of His sufferings were in His body. There were the marks on His hands, in His side, and on His body—the sign of His suffering.

- Now there is a strange thing in this verbiage, because John says the Lamb that he saw was standing. Standing, slain, destroyed, with blood poured out onto the earth.

- This has significant meaning because there Christ, the Lamb of God, *stands*, in the midst of the throne, preparing to receive the sovereignty of God's universe. He is standing on the basis of His sacrifice having identified Himself with us as our kinsman Redeemer; standing to take the purchased possession and to cast out Satan.

- He saw the Lamb standing in the majesty of the Lion, yet in the meekness and yieldedness of the Lamb. The picture of the Lamb is the picture of our Lord Christ in His first coming as they spit upon Him, but as He stands we see the significance of His second coming as the King of glory, when He will receive us back and bestow upon us full redemption of body, as well as soul and spirit.

- He stands—the Lion of the tribe of Judah, and the Root of David, who is the all-conquering, all-prevailing Lord.

- Notice also in verse 6 that John beheld there *"stood a Lamb as it had been slain, having seven horns and seven eyes."* The seven horns are representative of the fullness of power that has been placed in His hands. The seven eyes are representative of the knowledge, vigilance, and intelligence by which Christ takes care of His people—watching, directing, and counseling them concerning the final day, of which the Revelation here speaks, when He shall take unto Himself His great power and reign in the earth.

5. The Greatest Act
   - *"And he came and He took the book out of the right hand of him that sat upon the throne"* (5:7).
   - That is the greatest act in the entire story of God's creation, in the apocalypse, and in the history of mankind.
   - In other words, He lifted the title deed and He gave us back our lost inheritance.
   - In that act is the answer to the prayer of all of the saints through all the ages. In that act is the judgment of God upon sin, Satan, death, the grave, and hell.

6. A Doxology
   - The section of Scripture beginning with verse 8 could be called a doxology, a series of doxologies, or a psalm in heaven.
   - When He comes to take the book, all creation bursts into exuberance and triumphant joy. John describes the worship beginning in verse 8 and he describes three doxologies:
   a. First, the cherubim and the four and twenty elders lead off.
      - Notice first the worship of the redeemed. (See verse 8.) This is the climactic, all-meaningful moment when the Lamb of God is invested with the Kingship of the universe, and when the inheritance is to be bought back for Adam's fallen race.
      - This is when the Lamb, who alone is worthy, takes the book to break the seals. Then these four and twenty elders, who represent God's redeemed through the ages, bring to remembrance before the Almighty all that the prophets have spoken and all that God's saints have prayed.

- The burden of all our intercession is represented in the golden bowl in incense. All that the prophets have promise and said in comforting assurance is represented by the harp. The high priest has his bowl of incense; the prophet has his harp.

- Each elder also has a golden bowl of incense *"which are the prayers of the saints"* (verse 8). In temple worship, the high priest went into the holy sanctuary, as the people remained outside. The high priest carried a bowl of incense, and as the smoke and perfume of it ascended up to heaven, so the prayers of God's people were poured out before the throne of the Almighty.

b. Next, the worship of the angels. (5:11–12)

- Everywhere in the Word of God, angels are unnumbered. They are innumerable.

- The angels—in keeping with their inferior station of service (and it is not an astonishing thing that God's redeemed are greater than the angels—Hebrews 1), they do not address the Lamb directly when they speak to Him. They speak about Him, not to Him. They say, *"Worthy is the Lamb that was slain to receive power, and riches, and wisdom, and strength, and honour, and glory, and blessing"* (5:12).

- Another astonishing thing is that the angels never sing. Even though we refer to the angels singing, it is not true. Although we traditionally call our choirs the cherub choir or the celestial choir, the angels actually never sing.

- Always, people have spoken about the angels singing at the birth of Christ, but if you turn to Luke 2:13–14, you find *"and suddenly there was with the angel a multitude of the heavenly host praising God, and **saying**, Glory to God in the highest; on earth peace, good will toward men."*

- Is it thus here in the book of Revelation: "And I beheld, and I heard the voice of many angels…**saying** with a loud voice…" (5:11–12). Never in the Bible did the angels sing; they always *say*.

- Here there is a doxology. They are in a chorus, but it is what we would call a recitation or a speech chorus, for all together they say, but never does the Bible say that they sing.

- That's an astonishing thing. Always the redeemed sing. God's blood-washed throng always sings. Why not the angels?

- Music is made up of major chords and minor chords. Minor chords speak of the wretchedness, death, and sorrow, and most of nature moans and groans in a minor key. The sound of the wind, the sound of a storm, the sound of the ocean, and most sounds of nature are always in a minor key. The major key and major chords are chords of triumph and victory.

- He has put a new song in our souls and new praises on our lips, but an angel knows nothing of this. An angel has never been redeemed, and that's the only reason I can find that the angels never sing. It is God's people who sing. It takes a lost and fallen man who has been brought back to God, who has been forgiven of his sins, and who has been redeemed; it takes a saved soul to sing.

c. All of creation joins the worship.

- In verse 13, the doxologies grow in momentum and everything God has created joins in the song of adoration.

- Every created thing in the earth, in heaven, in the sea, and all in heaven and earth extol the Lord God.

- In verse 14, the four living creatures said *"Amen,"* and the redeemed, represented by the four and twenty elders, fell down and worshipped Him.

## How Much Do You Remember?

1. What is the significance of the book sealed with seven seals?
2. Who is able to open the book?
3. What is the significance of the word *"stood"* in John's description of the slain lamb?
4. Describe what is considered to be the greatest act of the apocalypse.
5. Name the three parts involved in the closing praise of this chapter.

## Your Assignment for Next Week:

1. Read chapter 6 of the book of Revelation.
2. Review your notes from this chapter.
3. Underline your Bible.

## Lesson 7 Notes

_____

_____

_____

_____

_____

_____

_____

_____

_____

_____

_____

_____

_____

_____

_____

_____

_____

_____

_____

_____

_____

# Lesson 8
# REVELATION 6

## The Tribulation Starts—The Beginning of Sorrows

1. *"And…when the Lamb opened one of the seals…"* (6:1).

   ✦ In Luke 4:20, Jesus closed the book after quoting from Isaiah 61:1–2, a fulfillment of prophecy of the first advent. Here, he opens this book telling of a second advent. Look up Luke 4:19–20:

   _____

   _____

   _____

   _____

   ✦ In Luke, He stopped reading at *"the acceptable year of the Lord,"* which is connected with this dispensation of grace.

   ✦ The day of vengeance of our God belongs to His second coming—to this second advent and to judgment.

2. The Start of the Judgments

   ✦ In chapters 4 and 5, we have seen a prologue setting the stage for the time of tribulation. The action concerning the tribulation begins here in chapter 6.

   ✦ Beginning here, we find that our Lord and Savior takes back our rightful inheritance from the hands of Satan. This is the beginning of the destruction of the powers of darkness and the bringing in of light, life, and everlasting righteousness.

   ✦ The seven seals include the proceedings of the Almighty after the church has been taken out of the earth and until they come back with the Lord and reign with Him.

   ✦ There are three groups of judgments: seals, trumpets, and vials or bowls. There are six seals of judgments, and the seventh seal opens the trumpets. There are six trumpet judgments, and the seventh trumpet opens the seven vial judgments. This makes a total of nineteen specific judgments that we will consider in our study of the book of Revelation.

   ✦ When they are finished, the judgment of God upon iniquity is finished. Then comes the binding of Satan and the establishment of the millennium in which God's children shall reign with Him in the earth.

3. The First Seal Opened (verses 1–2)

   ✦ You will note that as the seal is opened, one of the four beasts said, *"Come and see."* The word *"come"* can also mean "proceed" or "go," but in the King James Version, we have *"come and see,"* as though it is addressed to the apostle John.

4. The White Horseman

   ✦ Look up Revelation 6:2 to find the description of this horseman:

   _____

   _____

- The first horse described is in verse 2 is a white horse. You will notice that the one who sat on that horse had a bow and a crown, and he went forth conquering in order that he might conquer.

- In processions of triumph in ancient customs, the victor or conqueror always rode a white horse. In the nineteenth chapter of the book of Revelation, when our Lord returns from heaven, He comes riding a white horse. Those who follow him, God's people, blood-washed, victorious, follow Him on white horses.

- Therefore, practically all commentators will identify this rider of the white horse in Revelation 6 as Christ. But I have my doubts; here is why:

    a. There is a common denominator about the four horsemen of this chapter. They all ride across the stage of human history on horses—one white, one red, one black, and one greenish pale. Now, if the first one is Christ, then He is associated with one of the bloodiest and the most pestilential events our minds can imagine. I cannot connect the Lord Christ with the blood of war, the murder, and the death that follows the white horse.

    b. Another thing to consider: when Jesus Christ comes, He comes in Revelation 19:11 in its consummation and great final crowning, victorious day. We look for the Lord from heaven and so He does come with all of His people. His return does not occur here in the sixth chapter; it just does not fit.

    c. When comparing the two riders of white horses from Revelation 19 and 6, the Man who rides the white horse in chapter 19 has on His head *"crowns"* (verse 12), or a *diadema*, a Greek word never used for any other except the crown of a reigning, sovereign monarch. That is the kind of crown that one would expect to be on the brow of the Son of God. He comes with a crown and His weapon is the sword of the Word. But the white horseman in Revelation 6 is not so described. His crown is the Greek word *stephanos*—a garland or wreath, something a man could win on earth by being the victor in a race or a contest. He has in his hand not a sword of the Word of God, but a bow.

5. Comparing Matthew 24 with Revelation 6

    a. The outline

        - Our Lord has given us, in Matthew 24, an outline of this end time. If the Revelation is a picture of the end time, then it ought to fit exactly with the outline of our Lord in Matthew 24. Observe the outline in Matthew 24 starting at verse 4.

            1.) First, Jesus says, in answer to the question of the disciples as to what shall be the sign of His coming and of the end of the world: *"Take heed that no man deceive you. For many shall come in my name, saying, I am Christ; and shall deceive many"* (Matthew 24:4–5). The first thing the Lord says about this outline of history is that "there will be many false Christs."

            2.) The second thing He says in this outline is, *"And ye shall hear of wars and rumours of wars;…. For nation shall rise against nation, and kingdom against kingdom"* (verses 6–7). This is the red horse; the horse of blood.

            3.) The third thing He says in this outline is, *"and there shall be famines"* (verse 7). This is the black horse. Jeremiah says, in Lamentations 5:10, *"Our skin was black like an oven because of the terrible famine."*

            4.) The fourth thing Christ says, *"And there shall be…pestilences"* (verse 7). This is the fourth horse of death, following bloodshed, war, and famine.

    b. The horsemen identified

- If I can trust what the Lord says in Matthew 24, then I have the identification of these four horsemen of Revelation 6.
    - 1.) The first horseman represents the great deceiver; the great and final antichrist. The eyes of all the nations of the earth are upon him.
    - 2.) The second horseman represents the indescribable wars of the red horseman.
    - 3.) The third horseman is awful want and famine that inevitably goes with war.
    - 4.) The fourth horseman is pestilence and death—the grave swallowing up its unnumbered victims.

6. The Horses
   a. The white horse
      - First, the Lord says there will come on the scene the great deceiver, and he is Satan's masterpiece. Satan is a great imitator, so when he comes on this white horse, he imitates the Lord Christ here. As Christ is God's Man in the flesh, so Satan has his man.
      - His ultimate antichrist finally will appear when God's people are taken away and the days of the terrible tribulation begin. In the restlessness of nations, the revolution of the masses, and in the prospect of a catastrophic war, the first thing that will happen is the appearance of the great final dictator, as described in Revelation 6:1–2.
      - He will promise peace. He will bring with him every token of affluence and prosperity, and the nations and people of the earth will flock to him. He comes riding a white horse, conquering and to conquer. The entire military, economic, and political resources of the world will be at his disposal.
      - When we make this identification, we find that it will fit every prophecy in the Bible precisely. For example, in 2 Thessalonians 2:3–4, God says that after the falling away, and after God's people are taken away, the man of sin will be revealed. So this is the first thing that happens.
      - We have had a pattern of such men down through history as this antichrist. We have lived through some of them, called Hitler, Mussolini, Stalin, and many more. They all follow the same pattern, but are mere sketches of the great final antichrist. He will come first as the friend of humanity, the patron of the Roman Church, and a friend of the Jewish nation and people. He will give each one what they want and lead this world out of debt, war, and the restless revolution by which it ferments. He will lead them to great heights, on a white horse because he is the world's great dictator and the earth's sovereign leader.
      - Don't forget this first horse, the white horse, is the antichrist. Mark it in your Bibles beside Revelation 6:1–2 and Revelation 13:1–10.
   b. The red horse
      - The white horse is the leader, but he does not ride alone.
      - What inevitably follows is depicted here in the Revelation. The second of the living creatures said, *"Come and see"* (6:3). Then, *"there went out another horse that was red: and power was given to him that sat thereon to take peace from the earth, and that they should kill one another: and there was given unto him a great sword"* (6:4).
      - The red horseman represents not only nation rising against nation and kingdom against kingdom, but more nearly, the terrible slaughter of class against class and party against party as in a civil war. There is murder and bloodshed. The red horseman bathes the earth in blood.

- "*That they should kill one another...*"—Americans killing Americans, Frenchmen killing Frenchmen, and so forth. The whole world will be in a ferment of blood and revolution.

c.  The black horse

- Then comes the black horse in verses 5 and 6. This is the horse of famine. This represents worldwide financial catastrophe.

- With war spreading across the world, food, fuel, and other life supporting commodities will become more and more scarce.

- Notice in verse 5 that he that sat on the horse had a pair of balances, or a pair of scales, which indicates the scarcity of food, because the food shall be weighed out as carefully as gold.

- The frightening thing is that that day's ration of wheat will cost a penny, or a denarius, the biblical equivalent of an average worker's entire daily wage. (See Matthew 20:2.) Normally, a denarius would buy eight measures of wheat or twenty-four measures of barley. Under these famine conditions, the same wage will buy one measure of wheat or three of barley. In other words, there will be one-eighth of the normal food supply.

- The phrase "*see thou hurt not the oil and the wine*" is an ironic twist in this terrible situation. Apparently, luxury food items will not be in short supply, but of course most people will not be able to afford them.

- As this condition of soaring prices and the shrinking dollar continue to accelerate, it isn't hard to imagine how the world would come to the condition so graphically described here in Revelation 6:4–5.

d.  The pale green horse

- This fourth horse is the horse of death, found in verses 7 and 8.

- This is the same color that is described in the Old Testament as the color of leprosy.

- Notice that, in verse 8, he has the power to kill with the sword, with hunger, with death, and with beasts. It staggers the imagination to realize that one-fourth of the world's population will be destroyed within a matter of days. This will amount to billions of people!

- The means of extermination are four in number: 1: the sword (war), 2: hunger (famine), 3: death (plagues, infections, and diseases), 4: unrestrained beasts of the earth.

7.  The Martyr's Seal (Revelation 6:9–11)

a.  The fifth seal

- The opening of the second, third, and fourth seals are the judgments of God that follow the acceptance of the world dictator that is described in the first seal.

- Looking ahead, we will find that the sixth seal is a seal of the Judgment Day of God, and that the seventh seal is the seven trumpets of the judgments of God.

- With the opening of the fifth seal, we face something that most people shrink from—the knowledge that countless numbers shall suffer for their testimony with persecution and martyrdom during the tribulation.

- Those who become believers after the tribulation has started will be easy to identify. The antichrist will require that all men on earth worship him as God. All who refuse to profess his allegiance by receiving the antichrist's identifying mark will be prohibited from buying and selling. We find this in Revelation 14:9–11, which warns that all who do receive the mark of the beast will suffer at the hands of almighty God while those who do not receive it will suffer the wrath of the antichrist.

- The fifth seal is also a seal of judgment. Those who are martyred have born witness to the visitation of the wrath of God and, in their disembodied state, as souls, they cry for that day of vengeance.

- This fifth seal is different from the others in that we see not the action itself, but the result of action—the result of what has happened. In the other seals, as they are broken, we see the judgment develop as it occurs, but not here. This is the result of what has happened. John sees, under the altar, the souls of those who have already been slain.

b.  Who are these martyrs?

- Why are these martyrs' souls under the altar of heaven? As they cry to God, they ask, *"How long, O Lord, holy and true, dost thou not judge and avenge our blood on them that dwell on the earth?"* (6:10).

- So these martyrs are a special group, and their murderers still live on the earth. Therefore, these are not the martyrs of all times who have lost their lives in days throughout history. We know they are not the souls of those who have been martyred through all the ages because, in chapter 4, John sees the four and twenty elders around the throne of God's saints, and these four and twenty elders represent God's saints who have been raptured.

- These, then, are the martyrs who lost their lives under those first four seals in chapter 6—the first half of the tribulation.

- The martyrs of the last half of the tribulation are referred to in verse 11: *"And white robes were given unto every one of them; and it was said unto them, that they should rest yet for a little season, until their fellowservants also and their brethren, that should be killed as they were, should be fulfilled."* This is referring to those who are to be slain in the last half of the tribulation. Those who are under the altar are resting, waiting for the others to be slain.

- At the end of the great tribulation, and at the beginning of the millennium in Revelation 20:4, we shall find all of the martyrs standing in the presence of God and preparing to reign with the Lord for a thousand years.

- So these are they who have lost their lives under those terrible blood baths of the opening of the first four seals.

c.  The altar

- John says, *"I saw under the altar…"* (6:9).

- You know the story of the tabernacle, and like the earthly tabernacle, the heavenly tabernacle has two altars, both of which are described in the Bible.

- There is the altar of brass, which is the altar of sacrifice, and there is the altar of gold, which is the altar of burnt incense and prayer.

- The one we refer to here in our lesson is the altar of sacrifice, the brazen altar that stood in the courtyard of the tabernacle and of the temple.

- The Word of God always presents to all Christians the idea that we are to offer ourselves. We are to sacrifice ourselves for the Word and for the testimony of the Lord Jesus Christ. This idea can be found throughout Scripture.

- John says here, *"I saw under the altar the souls of them that were slain for the word of God."* In other words, the sacrifice had already been made and the action had passed; the life had been poured out.

d.  Why were these martyrs slain?

- They gave their lives for the Lord and the Lord looked upon them as His. They are His martyrs. They were slain *"for the word of God, and for the testimony which they held"* (6:9).

- In Revelation 1:9, it is said that John was exiled to Patmos *"for the word of God, and for the testimony of Jesus Christ."* But these are slain because of the Word of God and because of the testimony which they held. It is a little different. John was exiled for the Word and for the testimony of Jesus, but these were slain because of the Word of God and the testimony that they held on to.
- These are the martyrs who cry out to God. They have died for the cause of Christ.

e.   *"And they cried with a loud voice, saying, How long, O Lord, holy and true, dost thou not judge and avenge our blood on them that dwell on the earth?"* (6:10).

- And the answer to the martyrs' question is in verse 11, *"Rest yet for a little season, until [thy] fellowservants also and their brethren, that should be killed as [thy] were, should be fulfilled."*
- There is never a time when God does not have His true servants in the earth. They will be speaking, preaching, and declaring the Word of the Lord, and when these who are martyred are in heaven, God says to His martyrs in heaven: "Down there in that bloody earth, there are other fellow servants—thy brethren who are speaking the gospel of Christ and bearing witness to the truth of the Almighty. They are also to be killed; they shall be martyrs to the faith."
- All of this tragedy happens in the elected purpose of God. God has His book, and in His book are the names of those who are going to be martyred. God holds in His hands the suffering, the blood, and the fury, and yet, all of it is in God's plan.
- We may not fully understand why this is. Why this suffering? Why martyrs? We do not know, except that there is a mystery of evil that is known only to God. Our minds are finite, limited, but we know that God made us a people of choice. In the providence of God, and in the life and choice of the Almighty, it is decreed that we are allowed to suffer because of evil. That is why we have the Revelation; He is bringing in His righteous kingdom, and He is bringing in the great and final consummation of the new earth, new heaven, and new people.

8.   The Great Day of His Wrath (6:12–17)
- The sixth seal is not the end of history but the beginning of the end. It is a harbinger of that final consummating day.
- As I mentioned earlier, the book of Revelation follows in broad outline the twenty-fourth chapter of Matthew, which presents the apocalyptic discourse of our Lord. Our Lord in turn follows the pattern in the book of Daniel. In the ninth chapter of Daniel, the prophet divides the end of time into two equal parts—he calls it the seventieth week of Daniel. He divides the week that brings the end of the world into two halves, that is, three-and-a-half years to the first half and three-and-a-half years to the second half.
- Our Lord suggests that division of time in His apocalyptic discourse in Matthew 24:8–21. The first part He calls *"the beginning of sorrows"* (verse 8), and the last part He calls *"the great tribulation"* (verse 21).
- So we come to seal number six and the beginning of the end. This is the end of the first three-and-a-half years. This is the end of the beginning of sorrows. These first six seals then cover that period of time of the first half of that final week. The seventh seal opens the great tribulation.

a.   A brief recap, so that you can see the final build-up of how God works:
- The first seal introduces the final dictator, the man of sin. The history of these so-called rulers or saviors of the world is written in blood, tears, war, and death. After the antichrist and dictator come on the scene, war follows.

- The second horseman of the apocalypse is red. He has in his hand a great sword and the world is bathed in blood.

- The third horseman of the third seal follows after that on a black horse, and there is famine and want in the earth.

- The fourth horseman of the fourth seal follows with pestilence and the black plague. There is death, with graves opening to swallow up the vast multitude of humanity.

- Then seal number five is opened. With this seal, the action is not seen, but John beholds the souls of those who have been martyred for testimony of God and for the faith of Jesus that they held.

b. The sixth seal

- This sixth seal is the beginning of the final judgment of heaven. The rest of the book of Revelation describes the judicial administration of God as He deals with sin.

- In the sixth seal, there are these startling, paralyzing, and terrifying physical phenomena.

- The opening of the sixth seal is described in Revelation 6:12. Look up this verse:

_____

_____

_____

_____

- The Greek word *seismos*, meaning "quaking, shaking and agitating" is usually translated in the Bible, as it is in verse 12, as *"earthquake."* The underlying meaning of the word has reference to a hard shake. In the next verse, when the author likens the entire universe of God's creation to a fig tree, He says the tree will be shaken by a mighty wind. The Greek word for *"shaken," seio,* is derived from the same word previously translated as *"earthquake"* in verse 12.

- John continues his description of the opening of the sixth seal in verse 12, saying, *"and the sun became black as sackcloth of hair,"* black like a Bedouin's tent. When the Savior died, God's judgment fell upon our human sin. The whole sun was blotted out and there was darkness over the face of the earth. In the day of the judgment of God upon Egypt, there was a blackness of night that could be felt. It was dark, terrible, and terrifying. When the Lord came down at Mt. Sinai, the mountain was shrouded in blackness of smoke—a part of the sign of the judicial presence of God.

- John continues the description: *"and the moon became as blood."* The same description is found in Matthew 24:29. Look up this verse:

_____

_____

_____

_____

_____

_____

- John continues in verse 13: *"and the stars of heaven fell unto the earth."* John saw the earth and the whole creation as a fig tree that is shaken by a mighty wind. So God will shake this creation.

- *"And the heaven departed as a scroll when it is rolled together; and every mountain and island were moved out of their places"* (6:14). The configuration and the topography of this earth are changed when every mountain and every island are moved out of their places. What a day it will be!

c. What do these signs mean?

- We find these signs described exactly like that in the apocalyptic discourse of our Lord in Matthew 24. These things He described as the beginning of sorrows, and they are depicted here in the first six seals of the Revelation.

- He speaks of famines and pestilences, of wars and earthquakes. That is why the Lord Jesus spoke of it just as it is written here in the Revelation.

- Our Lord refers to the time when the sun shall be darkened and the moon shall not give her light, the stars shall fall from heaven, and the powers of the heaven shall be shaken: *"Then shall appear the sign of the Son of man"* (Matthew 24:30).

d. What do those who live on the earth do in that great judgment day of the Lord?

- The Bible says they are terrified—kings, great men, rich men, chief captains, mighty men, bondmen, and free men—all are terrified and hide themselves in the rocks and mountains. This can be read in verses Revelation 6:15–16.

- As they look upon what is happening, they use a phrase that is profound with eternal meaning: *"Hide us…from the wrath of the Lamb: for the great day of his wrath is come"* (6:16–17). What a phrase! For a lamb is gentle, a humble creature that one might carry in his arms, and yet, they say, *"the great day of his wrath is come."* God, the Lamb, the Savior who died for our sins, is also the Lord who is full of wrath and judgment toward those who spurn His overtures of grace and forgiveness.

- As the wrath of heaven grows more intense through the remainder of the judgments of God depicted in the book of Revelation, these evil men grow hard—very hard.

- Remember, judgment does not save a man. Only the grace of God can change a human heart and save a human soul. These condemned men under the sixth seal turned not to God who could save, but to the rocks to hide them from the face of Him who sits on the throne, and from the wrath of the Lamb—*"For the great day of his wrath is come; and who shall be able to stand?"* (6:17).

## How Much Do You Remember?

1. Briefly recap the events of chapter 6.
2. In this chapter, the judgments begin. When the first seal is opened, what do the beasts say?
3. Describe each horseman and what they represent.
4. Some say that the rider of the first horse, the white horse, is Christ. What are the reasons to believe this is not so, and who, in fact, is the rider?
5. How is the fifth seal, the martyr's seal, different from the rest of the seals?
6. Describe where the sixth seal falls in the division of time in the Lord's apocalyptic discourse from the book of Matthew.
7. What are some of the terrifying events that accompany the sixth seal?

## Your Assignment for Next Week:

1. Read Revelation chapter 7.
2. Write down any questions you have about chapter 7 as you read.
3. Review your notes from this lesson.
4. Underline your Bible.

## Lesson 8 Notes

_____

_____

_____

_____

_____

_____

_____

_____

_____

_____

_____

_____

_____

_____

_____

_____

_____

_____

# Lesson 9
# REVELATION 7

## An Interlude—The 144,000

- In chapter 7, we find a division into two parts. The first words found in verse 1 are, *"And after these things I saw...."* Then again in verse 9: *"After this I beheld [or I saw]."*

- The first vision concerns the children of Israel; the second vision concerns the great multitude of all kindred of peoples and tongues and concerns mainly the Gentiles.

- The picture here is vivid. All of the turbulence is held in abeyance for a brief time by the Lord God Almighty. We have seen the opening of the first six seals and some of the horror that has transpired upon the earth. This passage, this entire chapter, is an interlude, placed here between the opening of the sixth seal and the opening of the seventh seal.

- The seventh seal shall be opened at the beginning of chapter 8, but the beginning of that great and final tribulation period is broken between the *"beginning of sorrows"* and *"the great tribulation"* by this interlude.

1. The First Vision
- The first part of chapter 7 shall concern the 144,000 of all the tribes of the children of Israel. (See Revelation 7:1–8.)

- The chapter beings with John seeing four angels standing on the four corners of the earth, holding the four winds of the earth.

- We know that the number four is the number of the world, and here, we find a repetition of that number in these verses. The four angels standing on the four corners of the earth at the four quarters of the earth represent God's universal administration.

- The four angels in verse 1 have apparently been given authority over the weather conditions of the earth. The wind changes the pattern of all weather. Radical changes are taking place and shall continue to take place.

- You will note in verse 2: *"The four angels to whom it was given to hurt the earth and the sea."* This harm will be upon the earth, the sea, and the trees.

- Many of the prophecies relating to the tribulation indicate freak weather conditions and storms of unprecedented intensity. Jesus predicted these strange things regarding the relationship of the earth to the sun and moon and stars in Matthew 24, as well as in Luke 21. During this period, weather conditions will be changed radically.

2. Grace Before Judgment (verse 3)
- Before the angels are allowed to execute their judgment of shifting the wind patterns, another angel appears in verse 2. This angel has the seal of the living God with which He seals the special servants of God who will be His witnesses during the tribulation period.

- God has never allowed Himself to be without witnesses on earth to proclaim His way of receiving forgiveness and acceptance. The spiritual vacuum left by the removal of all true Christians at the rapture of the church will quickly be filled by these 144,000 Jewish *"servants of our God"* (7:3).

- The acts of sealing meant making an imprint in wax with a signet ring. This was done in ancient business transactions of all kinds and signified that whatever was thus sealed belonged to the one whose mark was on it. The idea of a visible mark of ownership and guarantee of protection is inherent in the Word of God.

+ In the New Testament, the seal of God is the Holy Spirit Himself. The seal of God—the Spirit—gives a special empowering to those servants to perform a particular mission. Revelation 7:3 speaks of a visible mark upon the forehead of the servants. Look up this verse:

_____

_____

_____

_____

+ You can be sure that this mark will be in direct contrast to the mark that the followers of the antichrist will receive when they swear allegiance to him. A person might be a "secret believer" today, but in those days, God's people will really be "marked people."

+ And so, for the sakes of these servants, this interlude here in chapter 7 is brought about by the Lord God. We find the mercy, grace, and love of God revealed to His elect.

3.  The Number—144,000 (verse 4)

    + This number of 144,000 is one of the symbolic numbers in the Bible, a number about whose identification there has been considerable argument.

    + For instance, one group (the Seventh Day Adventists) say that these 144,000 pertain to their own communion, who are found observing the Jewish Sabbath when the Lord comes again and they are raptured to glory.

    + Another group (the Jehovah's Witnesses) says that these 144,000 belong to them. They are to be saved at the end time. They are the great overcomers, and each one of these individuals is trying to be one of that select number. That is why you see them preaching on street corners and knocking on doors.

    + There are theologians by the hundreds who identify this group described in Revelation 7 as the true church. I feel this cannot be true because, for one thing, we have just seen the church, under the name of the redeemed, raptured to heaven, where they are crowned, robed, and enthroned.

    + For our study, we shall take the text just as it is written. This is what God said, so we will just accept it as meaning what He said. Look up Revelation 7:4 to know exactly what God said and meant:

_____

_____

_____

_____

+ The 144,000 are all of the tribes of the children of Israel.

+ The Bible says that the twelve thousand from each of the tribes of the children of Israel are to be sealed. In the Bible, the word *"twelve,"* with reference to the people of the Lord, always refers to Israel. Twelve is their number. There were twelve tribes.

+ So here are the twelve thousand sealed, elect, and called from the twelve tribes of the children of Israel.

+ That sealing is not a unique or particular thing because, all through the Bible, we find the Lord placing a mark, sealing those who belong to Him. In the days of Abraham, the mark was in the flesh with the rite of circumcision. In the days of exodus from Egypt, the mark was on the lintel above the door and on the door posts on either side. In the days of Rahab, it was a scarlet line hanging in the window. In Revelation 13, the antichrist has a mark that he puts on the right hands and on the foreheads of men. So the sealing, or marking, is not strange to the Bible.

4. Why Are These 144,000 Marked or Sealed?

- There are great spiritual reasons why God does as He does, and there are great spiritual reasons why God sealed these twelve thousand out of each of the tribes of Israel.

- They are chosen for a very definite reason, an elected purpose of God.

- In the sealing of the 144,000, they will be endued with Pentecostal power—and the Holy Spirit of God, in unction and in glory, will come upon them.

- What kind of seal will this be and how will it appear? How would you know that one of these men had been sealed of God? I think he would be much like Moses, when the Israelites saw him coming down from the mount after he had communed with God for forty days and forty nights. There was a glory about him; there was an unction about him and his face shown like the sun. I would say he would be like Stephen when he stood in the Sanhedrin amidst his murderers. They were not able to withstand the power and wisdom by which he spoke. That same glory shall be upon these 144,000.

5. What About the Difference in This List as Compared to Other Tribes Mentioned in Scripture?

- There seemingly are problems in this list of the twelve tribes of Israel.

  a. The first is the inclusion of Levi among the twelve tribes.

  - Normally, Levi, being the priestly tribe, was considered to have no inheritance among the twelve tribes. Perhaps he is included here because the priestly function ceased with the coming of Christ.

  b. The second problem is the mention of Joseph instead of Ephraim.

  - Normally, Manasseh and Ephraim are both mentioned, since they both received an equal portion of territory along with the rest of the tribes. Of course, twelve is counted in this list, but under the names of Joseph and Manasseh rather than Ephraim and Manasseh.

  c. The third problem concerns the omission of Dan from the list.

  - The usual reason given for this omission is that Dan was guilty of leading Israel into idolatry along with Ephraim. (See Leviticus 24:11; Judges 18:1–2; 1 Kings 12:28.)

  - It is suggested by many that the antichrist may come from this tribe of Dan and that this accounts for its omission from this list. Whatever the reason for Dan's omission from the tribes from which the 144,000 shall come, this is not the end of God's dealing with that tribe.

  - The Danites will receive a portion of the land during the millennial kingdom. Indeed, in Ezekiel 28:1, Dan heads the list of the tribes as the inheritance is divided to them.

  - Individual members of these tribes can certainly be brought into God's kingdom by faith, but they shall not be given a party of that great evangelistic endeavor during the tribulation.

6. How Are the 144,000 Converted?

- You might ask, "If all the Christians are taken out of the world in rapture, how are these evangelists going to be saved?" There are several ways:

  a. Some Jews will have been witnessed to by Christian friends and will surely have heard something about prophecy relating to the disappearance of the church.

  b. Others will surely be perplexed by the strange phenomenon of missing people and will not accept the reasons given by various satanically inspired groups. They will seek an honest answer.

+ It is important to remember that the Holy Spirit will still function in His role of drawing people to Jesus, however, He will relate to believers as He did during the Old Testament times. He will regenerate the human spirit of those 12,000 from the twelve tribes and will indwell and empower them for special service.

7. The Blood-Washed Multitude—The Second Vision (verses 9–17)

+ Now we come to some of the results of the work of the 144,000 Jewish preachers.

+ Notice, in verse 9, John says, "*After this* [after this selection and after the sealing] *I beheld, and, lo, a great multitude, which no man could number, of all nations, and kindreds, and people, and tongues, stood before the throne, and before the Lamb, clothed with white robes, and palms in their hands.*"

+ You may be asking, "Who are the uncounted numbers of this multitude, and where do they come from?" You find the answer by reading the Scripture and taking the whole text together. The pertinent key to these Scriptures is found in verses 13–14.

+ John had not said anything and there is no recorded conversation, yet one of the elders answered, saying that he recognized John's perplexity and astonishment as to the great multitude. And so, the elder speaks what John was thinking: "Who are these people arrayed in white robes?" And John said, "Sir, I do not know."

+ For if this multitude represents the church, the saved, the redeemed of Christ, there would have been no complexity on the part of John.

+ Thus, the 144,000 sealed from the twelve tribes *are not* the same group that is described beginning here in verse 9. These are two distinct and separate groups. Neither are they the church, and let me illustrate why:

 a. The church was *kept* out of great tribulation (3:10). This multitude *came* out of great tribulation (7:14).
 b. The church shall sit on thrones around the throne; these stand before the throne (7:9, 15).
 c. The church wears crowns; these are uncrowned.
 d. The church will have harps and vials (5:8); these have palms in their hands (7:9).
 e. The church shall sing a new song; these cry with a loud voice (7:10).
 f. The church shall be kings and priests and reign with Him (1:6, 20:6); these serve Him day and night (7:15).

+ And so, the words, "*These are they which came out of great tribulation*" (7:14) are very meaningful. These, then, are tribulation saints. These are the ones whom God has saved, in His mercy, during those dark days.

+ Even in those dark and tragic days, in wrath, God remembers mercy. He elects 144,000 and seals them, empowers them for that awful and final day. There are those who, listening to these preachers, turn in faith to the Messiah and wash their robes and make them white in the blood of the Lamb.

+ Three different times in this short passage, their white robes are mentioned (7:9, 13, 14). The Greek word *stola* refers to an outer garment, worn for dignity, grace, beauty, and distinction. That's the same word used here and we use it today for the word *stole*. Here, it refers to the outer garment worn by God's blood-bought who are washed clean and pure. The basis of their faith is the fact they have looked in faith, repentance, and trust to the atoning Lamb of God.

+ The palm branches in their hands is an Old Testament reference to the feast of the tabernacle, when the prophets sat in booths and carried palm branches, called to remember God's deliverance out of the darkness of servitude of Egypt. In Nehemiah 8:17, the people are also rejoicing over the deliverance from Babylonian captivity, praising God with palm branches in their hands.

+ Notice, in verses 15–16, that these multitudes are before the throne of God and that they serve Him day and night. And then, in verse 16, we find some negatives, such as, *"They shall hunger no more, neither thirst any more; neither shall the sun light on them, nor any heat."* These negatives are often used in the Revelation. In Greek, the more negatives used, the more emphatic the meaning of the message.

+ These tribulation saints are not to be compared to those who are a part of the bride of Christ, those of us in this day of grace who have the opportunity to accept Christ now.

+ The church is the enthroned elders. As believers today, we have an opportunity to be among those enthroned elders. It is much better to be a king than a servant, better to be sitting on a throne than standing before a throne, better to have a crown on your head than a palm branch in your hand. Likewise, it is better for us now to have the opportunity to be before the enthroned presence of God as a part of the bride of Christ, a member of the church, than to be one of the 144,000 tribulation saints.

+ This is our present opportunity. The tribulation saints will missed it and had to wait until being plunged into the flood and the bloodbath of a great judgment. Out of the sorrow, trial, and martyrdom, they were brought up to heaven to stand in the presence of God. They are never a part of the enthroned elders, or the true bride of Christ. They will be the guests of the bride and Bridegroom. That's the difference between the dispensation of grace and the work of God after the church has been called out.

## How Much Do You Remember?

1. How many parts or visions make up chapter 7 and what do they concern?
2. Why is this chapter considered "an interlude"?
3. What does the number 144,000 represent and why are they sealed?
4. Who are the multitude in the second vision and how are they described?

## Your Assignment for Next Week:

1. Read Revelation chapter 8.
2. Review your notes from this lesson.
3. Underline your Bible.

## Lesson 9 Notes

_____

_____

_____

_____

_____

_____

_____

_____

_____

_____

_____

_____

_____

_____

_____

_____

_____

_____

_____

_____

_____

# Lesson 10
# REVELATION 8

## The Trumpet Judgments – Part One

1.  The Seventh Seal (verses 1–6)

    + The seventh and final seal, you will recall, opens the seven trumpet judgments.

    a.  The silence

        + In verse 1, at the opening of the seventh seal, all of heaven becomes quiet.

        + When the Lamb opened the first seal, there was a voice of thunder, saying, *"Come."* When the Lamb opened the second, third, and fourth seals, that same thunderous voice was heard. When the Lamb opened the fifth seal, John heard the cry of those who were martyred for Christ and saw their souls under the altar. When the Lamb opened the sixth seal, there was a great tremor throughout all the framework of nature.

        + When the Lamb now opens the seventh and last seal, we see that there is silence for a period of one half-hour. This is a stillness and a silence of expectancy, for this is the last seal. It is also a silence that precedes the onslaught of terrible judgment yet to come.

        + Silence, at this point, after all of the expressions of the six seals, would be an awesome thing, because this is the beginning of the last drama of the ultimate mystery of almighty God. It seems as though the Lord God Himself pauses before the onward rush of this great, final, judicial administration.

        + The silence in heaven at the opening of the seventh and last seal, brings to view the drama of the great tribulation.

    b.  After the silence—the seven trumpets

        + The first thing the apostle John sees after the silence is the seven angels who stand in the presence of God.

        + These seven are a distinct, select, administering group of angels who carry out the instructions of the Lord God.

        + To these seven angels, the Lord God gives seven trumpets. The trumpet is given because it is the most used of all the instruments of the Holy Scripture and portrays the life of the people in the presence of God. For example, if there is a war declared, there is the blowing of the trumpet. In the great convocations of the people of God, there was the sounding of the trumpet. This also took place at all of the great festival days and in the crowning of a king.

    c.  *"Another angel came"* (8:3)—who was this angel?

        + At least four times in the Revelation, that identical designation of *"another angel"* is used, always with reference to a mighty, glorious personality in heaven. (See Revelation 7:2; 8:3; 10:2; 18:1.)

        + Here, in Revelation 8:3, this angel stands at the altar, and in his hand is the golden censer, which alone belongs to the priest.

        + Because of these descriptions, and especially because of his priestly ministry, many students of the Word of God say that this angel is the Lord Jesus Christ. I have no objection to those who interpret Scripture as meaning this, but I have this observation to make: everywhere in the apocalypse that our Lord appears—He is distinctly designated. In the first chapter,

He is called *"the Son of man"* (1:13). In the fifth chapter, He is called *"the Lion of the tribe of Judah, the Root of David"* (5:5), and in the next verse, *"a Lamb as it had been slain"* (5:6). In the nineteenth chapter, He is called *"The Word of God"* (19:13).

- ✦ The Lord Christ is always distinctly designated, but here, and in other like passages in Revelation, the phrase used is *"another angel,"* which leads me to believe that this is an angel-priest, and that we should refer to him as such.

- ✦ While these seven, select angels of God stand ready to sound, there appears this angel-priest standing at the great burnt offering of sacrifice.

- ✦ Both altars of the heavenly temple are mentioned here in verse 3. The angel-priest, standing in the court, fills his golden censer with the fire from the brazen altar, and with incense, offers it at the golden altar before the throne.

- ✦ The traditional Jewish tabernacle worship scene included an outer court with a brazen altar of sacrifice, where all sacrifices were offered up to God in a fire that never died, and an inner holy place before the veil, the great altar of incense with its four golden horns, one at each corner. These are the two altars: the brazen altar of sacrifice and the golden altar of prayer. Both are referenced in this verse.

- ✦ Here in Revelation 8:3–5, the angel-priest stands at the brazen altar of sacrifice, filling his censer with the fire from the altar. He then proceeds to the holy place, putting incense on the coals of fire. He offers the incense with the prayers of all the saints. These saints included the saints of the tribulation days—and they may also include the saints of all time, whose longing petitions for the coming of the kingdom of the Lord are now about to be answered.

- ✦ After prayer ascends—notice what happens in verse 5. The angel fills his censer with fire from the altar (not the golden altar before the throne, but the brazen altar of judgment) and he casts it in to the earth. There follows a token judgment: voices, thunder, lightning, and an earthquake—a foretaste of the judgment to follow.

- ✦ Notice that this angel-priest takes the golden censer, filled with incense that ascends unto God—a picture of the devotion, love, hope, prayers, and intercession of judgment.

- ✦ He then fills his empty censer with fire from the coals off the altar of brass, but this time he flings the censer into the earth, where it scorches, burns, and it consumes. The same censer that sent prayer of incense in the worship at the golden altar is used to reveal judgment on the part of God.

- ✦ As he casts the fire into the earth, what follows is the inevitable judgment of God upon a blaspheming, rejecting, unbelieving earth.

2. The First Four Trumpets (8:7–13)

- ✦ As we enter the study of the trumpet judgments, you will notice that these seven judgments are divided into four and three; the first four are in a series to themselves; the last three are in a series to themselves and are called "woes."

- ✦ These first four are general judgments upon the earth; the last three judgments are directly pointed toward mankind. They increase in intensity and severity as they follow through.

   a. The first trumpet (verse 7)

   - ✦ The first trumpet will bring hail and fire, mingled with blood, on earth.

   - ✦ The result will be the burning of a third part of the earth. One third of all the vegetation will be burned up.

   - ✦ With the massive loss of vegetation will come floods and erosion. But even as God judges, He is also gracious, because He leaves two thirds of the greenery untouched.

b.  The second trumpet (verses 8–9)

   ·  The instrument of the second judgment is described *"as it were a great mountain burning with fire."*

   ·  John does not say what the instrument of judgment will be, but he clearly reveals the after-effects of the judgment.

   ·  A third part of the sea will become blood, causing the death of a third part of the life in the sea and a third part of the shipping vessels.

c.  The third trumpet (verses 10–11)

   ·  The judgment of the third trumpet affects the freshwater supply of the world. It becomes bitter, resulting in many deaths.

   ·  The instrument of judgment will be a great star labeled Wormwood.

   ·  Many species of wormwood live in Israel. All have a strong, bitter taste, leading many to use the plant as a symbol of bitterness, sorrow, and calamity throughout all of Israel.

   ·  The water of this judgment will be so bitter and poisonous that many people will die, either from drinking it or from thirst.

d.  The fourth trumpet judgment (verses 12–13)

   ·  The fourth judgment will affect the sun, moon, stars, and the uniformity of the day/night cycle.

   ·  The sun, moon, and stars will be smitten to the extent of one third, with the result that the now twenty-four-hour cycle will be shortened to a sixteen-hour cycle.

   ·  The Lord Himself predicted, in the Olivet Discourse, these certain signs in Luke 21:25. Look up this verse:

   _____

   _____

   _____

   _____

At this point, you can imagine the consequences of losing one-third of all vegetation, marine life, and shipping. Add to that the poisoning of one-third of the world's water resources, and then the curtailment of natural light by one-third, and you can see that the rapid succession of all of these judgments is designed by God to shock man into changing his mind about the Lord Redeemer.

3.  The Announcement of Woes (verse 13)

   ·  At this point, John hears and sees an angel, flying through heaven and announcing woes upon the earth.

   ·  Notice the angel says, *"Woe, woe, woe...."* Three times the angel repeats this because there are three woes yet to come, and they are under the fifth, sixth, and seventh trumpets.

   ·  This is specifically directed at the inhabitants of the earth.

   ·  As terrible as the first four trumpet judgments shall be, the last three shall be worse, and, therefore, they are designated as woes. Before entering into these woes. we must stop and consider the warning here that trumpets five, six, and seven will bring a new quality and degree of disaster.

   ·  We shall see the first woe in the locusts, the second in the Euphrates horsemen and the plagues wherewith the two witnesses smite the earth. The third we see in the handing over of the earth to the beast worship, which is the worst, by far, of all.

## How Much Do You Remember?

1. What does the opening of the seventh seal open?
2. What is the atmosphere like after the seventh seal is opened?
3. Who is the *"other angel"* spoken of in Revelation 8:3?
4. How are the trumpet judgments grouped or divided?
5. Describe judgments 1–4. What are the results of these?

## Your Assignment for Next Week:

1. Read Revelation chapter 9.
2. Review your notes from this lesson.
3. Underline your Bible.

## Lesson 10 Notes

_____

_____

_____

_____

_____

_____

_____

_____

_____

_____

_____

_____

_____

_____

_____

_____

_____

_____

# Lesson 11
# REVELATION 9

## The Trumpets of Woe upon the Earth

1.  The Fifth Trumpet—The First Woe (verses 1–12)

    a.  The fallen star

    + The *"star"* of Revelation 9:1 is easy to identify. The wording is clear if we read the passage from a literal standpoint. *"I saw a star fall from heaven unto the earth: and to him was given the key of the bottomless pit."* In verse 11, we read, *"And they had a king over them, which is the angel of the bottomless pit."* He apparently is the same creature in both verses, which identifies him as Satan.

    + You will note in verse 2 that when this *"star,"* which we have identified as Satan, opens the bottomless pit, *"there arose a smoke out of the pit, as the smoke of a great furnace; and the sun and the air were darkened by reason of the smoke of the pit."*

    b.  The locusts

    + Then. in verse 3: *"There came out of the smoke locusts upon the earth."* You may wonder where these locusts come from. They come from the bottomless pit. Luke 8:31 also refers to the abode of the demons as *"the deep."*

    + When Satan opens the pit, smoke ascends as the smoke from a great furnace. These locusts described as coming out of the pit are possessed with demonic attributes.

    + As we read verses 3 through 6, it is clear that these are not ordinary locusts, and their origin is from that bottomless pit.

    + These creatures are described as being real, so we must not consider them as merely symbolic representations and judgments.

    + They are animal creatures, like locusts, though not ordinary locusts, for they are demonic in nature. Indeed, it would be better to describe them as demons who take the form of these unique locusts.

    + The destruction that these demons inflict is described in verse 3 as *"like that of scorpions."* In his book, *The Apocalypse*, J. A. Seiss states:

    > The pain from the sting of a scorpion, though not generally fatal, is perhaps the intensest that any animal can inflict upon the human body. The insect itself is the most irascible and malignant that lives, and its poison is like itself. Of a boy stung in the foot by a scorpion [it was related that]…he rolled on the ground, grinding his teeth, and foaming at the mouth…. Such is the nature of the torment which these locusts from the pit inflict. They are also difficult to be guarded against, if they can be warded off at all, because they fly where they please, dart through the air, and dwell in darkness.[1]

    + In verses 4 and 5, God places certain limitations upon the activity of these demons. They will be limited as to what they may strike, how far they may go, and how long they may do

1. J. A. Seiss, *The Apocalypse: Lectures on the Book of Revelation* (New York: Cosimo Inc., 2007), 206.

it. They will not attack the vegetation of the earth (as common locusts do); they may only attack certain men—that is, those who have not the seal of God on their foreheads.

- The wicked will persecute God's servants—the 144,000—but, in turn, they will be tormented by this plague, which God allows.

- The demon-locusts will also be limited in that they may not kill men, only torment them.

- The duration of this particular plague will be five months, as stated in verses 5 and 10.

- In verse 6, we find that the effect of this torment by locusts will drive men to suicide but they will not be able to die. Although men will prefer death to the agony of living, death will not be possible.

- In verses 7–12, we find a description of the locusts.

- Overall, they are like horses prepared for battle. On their heads are, as it were, crowns of gold. Their faces are as the faces of men, and their hair as the hair of women. Their teeth are as those of lions and they have breastplates of iron. The scorpion-like sting of their tails is mentioned again, along with the duration of the plague for five months.

- The power of demons is great and these uncommon locusts are demonic and controlled by Satan.

- Although this judgment is literally hell on earth, the overruling power of God is interwoven throughout this passage. He allows judgment to occur; He sets the limit on the destructive power of these locusts; He brings it to a conclusion when His purpose is fulfilled. He is in complete control.

- These creatures are led in their work by a king, Satan. His name is given both in Hebrew and Greek in verse 11, both meaning "destroyer." In this judgment, Satan, through his demons, will attempt to destroy the bodies of men.

c. The great announcement

- In verse 12, there is a great announcement. Look up this verse:

_____

_____

_____

- Here, we are given the pronouncement that one woe has finished and two more are still to come.

- This verse helps us keep the three woes separate from each other. They never run concurrently, always one after the other.

2. The Second Woe—The Sixth Trumpet (verses 13–21)

- In verse 13, the voice of this first angel mentioned here belongs to the same angel-priest introduced in Revelation 8:3. He commands the trumpet angel to loose four angels that were bound in the Euphrates River.

a. The Euphrates

- Here is one angel, under the command of the angel-priest, loosing four evil angels, who, up to this time, had been bound in the Euphrates River. This is especially momentous.

- The first human sin was committed at this Euphrates—in the garden of Eden. In this area, the first murder and the first great revolt against God took place. It was in nearby Babylon that the first world ruler set up his kingdom. The Euphrates region is truly the site of many significant events of human history. The Euphrates was considered by the Romans, Greeks, and Babylonians as the dividing line between east and west.

b. The four angels

- These four angels were prepared for the hour, the day, the month, and the year they had been waiting for.

- The purpose of their release is to kill a third of the human race (9:15).

- Again, one sees the sovereign hand of God working all these events in His own timing. These demons, who had been kept for this hour, could not have been released or freed by Satan until God gave the command.

- Under the fourth seal judgment in Revelation 6:8, one fourth of the earth had already been slain. Now one third is to be killed. This means that these two judgments alone—to say nothing of the death caused by other wars and pestilence—have reduced the population of the earth by one-half.

- When those four angels are loosed—they have a method, a way to kill one third of the population. So they, in turn, loose an army of torment and destruction, and the number of that army is to be two hundred million (9:16).

- This army is considered by some to be composed of actual human beings and by others as being an army of demons. Some believe that the two hundred million soldiers described here will be from east of the Euphrates.

- John describes, in verse 17, what he saw. It is not be any more difficult to interpret that verse as demonic as we did the locusts of the first woe.

- The weapons of this army are fire, smoke, and brimstone—the weapons of hell. This further indicates that the army is made up of the inhabitants of hell—demons.

c. Consequences of the sixth trumpet

- The consequences of this sixth trumpet will be found in verses 18-21. *"By these three"* should read "by these three plagues"; that is, fire, smoke, and brimstone.

- The first consequence of the activity of this army is that one third of the population is destroyed.

- The second consequence concerns those who are not killed. One would expect that in the midst of all this suffering, men would turn to God and cry out for mercy. Instead, we read that they *"repented not"* (9:20). In verses 20–21 is a description of the religion and life of unredeemed man on the earth during these tribulation days. His religion will be the worship of demons and idols. The two sadly fateful message of this lesson is found in verses 20–21. Look up these verses:

_____

_____

_____

_____

_____

_____

_____

_____

- They not only hold on to worshipping idols, but they will not repent of the four main sins that take place during these tribulation days.

- In verse 21, we find the list of the four most prominent sins during this time. The significance of these particular sins is great in the light of present trends in the world. It is no coincidence that the four major sins listed here are four of the most serious problems facing us today.

- These four sins are murder, occult activities or *"sorceries"* (stemming from the Greek word *pharmika*, which means pharmacy but refers here to the practice of the occult with the use of drugs), fornication, and burglary.

- Notice that three of these four practices are direct violations of three of the Ten Commandments: murder, fornication, and stealing. Vice will reign in the place of virtue.

- All of these are signs of what shall be during the tribulation period.

3. An Interlude

- Now, at the close of chapter 9, we see another interlude.

- This shall be the longest interlude by far. So, before we come to the seventh trumpet, God has given a little time—which we call an interlude—and then, in Revelation 11:13, we pick up the final two verses of the second woe and enter into the seventh trumpet.

## How Much Do You Remember?

1. Who is the fallen star found in verse 1?
2. Describe the locusts that emerge from the pit. What other creature will their destruction be likened to?
3. What are the locusts limited to and how long will that plague be permitted to last?
4. Describe the second woe.
5. Where will the four angels emerge from and why is this area significant?
6. Approximately how much of earth's population will have been slain after this sixth trumpet judgment?
7. What are the weapons of the army of this second woe?
8. What are the consequences of this sixth trumpet?

## Your Assignment for Next Week:

1. Read Revelation chapter 10.
2. Review your notes from this lesson.
3. Underline your Bible.

## Lesson 11 Notes

_____

_____

_____

_____

_____

_____

_____

_____

_____

_____

_____

_____

_____

_____

_____

_____

_____

# Lesson 12
# REVELATION 10

This passage is part of the longest interlude between the series of judgments.

All three of the series of judgments are framed exactly alike—the series of the seven seals, the seven trumpets, and the seven bowls (or vials) of the wrath of God.

Between the sixth and seventh judgements there is an interlude. Between the sixth and seventh seals, the seventh chapter of the book of Revelation, is an interlude. Between the sixth and seventh bowls, Revelation 16:13–16, is an interlude. In this series of the trumpet judgments, between the sixth and seventh trumpets, we find an interlude that extends from Revelation 10:1–11:13.

1. The Finished Mystery of God (verses 1–7)

   a. The angel

   - In Revelation 10:1, we read, *"And I saw another mighty angel come down from heaven…."*

   - Most scholars agree that this great angel is none other than a description of our Lord Jesus Christ, however, I do not think this is so. The description is appropriate for a full ambassadorial representative of our Lord.

   - I do not think this angel is the Lord Jesus because this angel appears all through the book of Revelation. (See Revelation 5:2; 7:2; 8:3; 18:1; and here, 10:1.) To me, these are all the same angel. If he is but an angel, he is certainly some glorious creation of God who serves and administers before the throne of heaven. Some commentators say that this angel is Michael, the archangel—his name means "one like God."

   - This angel of the Lord God set one foot upon the sea and one foot on land, and declared that those things belong to God. When a man sets his foot on something, it means he is possessing it. We also find this when God addresses His people in Deuteronomy 11:24. Look up this verse:

   _____

   _____

   _____

   _____

   - The cry of the angel was with a loud voice like the roaring of a lion. This would indicate the strength of the angel's voice.

   b. The mystery

   - Two things happen after the loud voice: first, *"seven thunders uttered their voices"* (10:4); second, John is restrained from revealing what the thunders say.

   - Thunder always points toward storms, but the specific details are not revealed here, only a voice from heaven forbidding John to write down what he had heard.

   - In verse 7, we find the heart of the first part of chapter 10: *"But in the days of the voice of the seventh angel* [the last trumpet judgment—the last woe], *when he shall begin to sound, the mystery of God should be finished, and he hath declared to his servants the prophets."*

- The *"mystery of God"* is the long delay of our Lord in taking the kingdom to Himself and in establishing righteousness in the earth.
- There is an elected time when that angel shall sound and the kingdom of this world shall become the kingdom of our God and His Christ.
- The idea in verse 7 is that there should no longer be an interval of time, that is, a delay, because the mystery of God will be finished when that seventh angel sounds—which opens the last series of the judgments of God.
- According to this verse, these are the good tidings that God has declared—evangelized—to His servants, the prophets. The Greek phrase translated as *"declared to...the prophets"* is meaningful. Always in the message of the prophets, good tidings are announced. The prophet may see the storm, the furor, the battle, and the conflict, and his writings may be filled with woe and lamentations, but the prophet always saw the glorious day dawning—always. That is why John uses the word *"declared,"* which actually means "evangelized."
- The key to interpretation of verse 7 is in the inclusion of the last few words of verse 6: *"There should be [delay] no longer: but in the days of the voice of the seventh angel...."* Thus, we know that the mystery of God will be finished when the seventh angel sounds and opens the last series of judgments of God.

2. The Bittersweet Book (verses 8–11)
   a. The angel
      - This angel, clothed with a cloud, a rainbow upon his head, with his face as the sun and his feet like pillars of fire, sets one foot upon the sea and one foot upon the land and, in the name of the Lord God, claims all creation for the Almighty.
      - He lifts his right hand to heaven and swears by God, who lives forever, that the delay of the mystery of God is to be finished in the days of the sounding of the next trumpet. He has in his hand a little book. (See verse 8.)
      - John becomes an actor in the drama for the first time and is commanded to eat the book. When he does so, it is as honey in his mouth and as gall in his stomach. Next, the Lord says that the apostle, having digested the words of the book, is to deliver it to the peoples, nations, tongues, and kings.
   b. The seven thunders
      - When the angel, who had in his hand the open little book, begins to speak, it is as a lion reading. All of God's creation hears his voice and after he speaks, seven thunders utter their voices in reply.
      - John says that when those thunders uttered their voices, he was about to write what had been said, but a voice from heaven said, *"Seal up those things which the seven thunders uttered, and write them not"* (10:4).
      - John carried whatever had been said to him to the grave. We do not know what these voices of God said, but we know from their number, and from the fact that they are thunders, that the words *"seven thunders"* means something. Just as there are seven lamps, seven spirits of God, seven seals, seven trumpets, and seven vials, there are also seven thunders, representing the entire magnitude and fullness of the pronouncement of God.
   c. The book
      - In Revelation 5:1, John saw a book in the hand of God. Now, in chapter 10, when you find the same Greek word translated as *"little book,"* you might suppose this is a different book. However, I believe they are the same, for the same word is used to describe both of them.

- The difference is that in Revelation 5, the book was sealed with seven seals, whereas here, the book in the angel's hand is open. This is important to remember.

- The book in the hand of God was sealed with seven seals, but now, in the tenth chapter, all seven of those seals have been broken and the little book is completely open. The sealed book represents a forfeited inheritance. The breaking of those seals represents the redemption of that inheritance and the casting out of Satan.

- The angel now gives the little book to John (see verse 9) and the angel says that he should take it and eat it. That refers to a plain and simple thing that we often find in the Word of God. To "eat it up" is to assimilate it, digest it, and get it into our soul. As Jeremiah said, in Jeremiah 15:16, "O Lord, thou knowest…. Thy words were found, and I did eat them."

- John was to eat this book and then prophesy before the prophets, nations, tongues, and kings of the earth. So John did just that. He took the Word of God, he took the revelation of the Almighty, and he ate it. It was sweet like honey in his mouth and like bitter like gall in his stomach.

- Herein is one of the most profound truths to be found in Scripture. The apocalypse itself, the unveiling, is like that. The sweetness of this little book, the apocalypse, can easily be verified and seen in the great mass of apocalyptic literature that has grown up around it, but there is no student of the Word of God who has ever sought to understand these prophetic messages, but that he finds in them the terrible violence of the coming storm. The apocalypse describes a bitter future.

- All of the blessings of God are sweet to all of us, but to people who refuse God's admonitions, the words are bitter as gall.

- What we have seen is the fact that some of the revelations of God may be pleasant to the taste, and yet, the contemplation or digestion of the truth may bring heaviness.

- Too often, when one enters into an understanding of things to come, he never gets beyond the tasting stage. But when one digests all of the truth of judgment that is yet to come, it can only bring heaviness of heart to the child of God.

- Finally, John is commissioned by a voice in verse 11 that he must prophesy again. Full of the sweet taste and bitterness of the little book, necessity was laid upon him to preach and to prophesy. Notice that this prophecy will concern many people and nations and tongues and kings.

- Remember that this interlude continues up through Revelation 11:12. We shall look at chapter 11 and study the temple and the two witnesses. Before reading it, however, I suggest you read Daniel 9. The two chapters go hand-in-hand because we study that time period that is so important in Daniel's seventieth week.

- The climax of the sixth trumpet (the second woe) will not be completed until we get to verses 13 and 14 of the eleventh chapter. It is of utmost importance that you remember where we are in the judgments, and that we are now studying the interlude that takes place between the sixth and the seventh trumpets.

## How Much Do You Remember?

1. In all three series of judgments (seals, trumpets, and bowls), what comes between the sixth and seventh judgment?
2. Describe the cry of the angel from Revelation 10:3.
3. What was John restrained from writing down?
4. What is the *"mystery of God"* found in this chapter?
5. What is John commanded to eat and how does it taste? What is he to do following its consumption?
6. Describe the difference between the book mentioned in chapter 5 and chapter 10.

## Your Assignment for Next Week:

1. Read Revelation 11 and Daniel 9.
2. Review your notes from this lesson.
3. Review the order and outline of the judgments we have already studied in order to keep in remembrance where we are in the progression.
4. Underline your Bible.

## Lesson 12 Notes

_____

_____

_____

_____

_____

_____

_____

_____

_____

_____

_____

_____

_____

_____

_____

_____

_____

_____

# Lesson 13
# REVELATION 11

## The Temple—The Two Witnesses and the Trumpet

1. The Interpretation, Time, and Place of Chapter 11 (verses 1–8)

   + Most scholars will say that this chapter is, undoubtedly, the most difficult chapter in all of the book of Revelation. The interpretations of this present passage are confusing and oftentimes inconclusive.

   + There are a multitude of thoughts and ideas from various scholars, but as we have prayed and studied, I do not think that God intends for us to presuppose or to have personal viewpoints, but instead, to merely see the will and the elected purpose of God in revealing to us the whole counsel of God.

   + If you read the text carefully, the first impression you will get is that we are distinctly and unmistakably on Jewish ground. Look at verse 8: *"Their dead bodies shall lie in the street of the great city, which spiritually is called Sodom and Egypt…."*

   + John continues, *"…where also our Lord was crucified."* Our Lord was not crucified in Damascus, Memphis, or Thebes. Our Lord, our Savior, was crucified in Jerusalem.

   + The apostle describes the sinfulness of that city by saying that spiritually it is Sodom in its sin, and spiritually it is Egypt in its worldliness. John definitely says that he is talking about Jerusalem.

2. The Holy City, Jerusalem

   + Look up verse 2:

   _____

   _____

   _____

   _____

   + *"The holy city"* is a word, an expression that is used in the Bible for only one city alone. There is no other city on earth that is called the holy city except Jerusalem.

   + The only exception is found in Revelation 21:10, where the New Jerusalem is called *"the great city, the holy Jerusalem, descending out of heaven from God,"* and certainly it will never be trampled by the armies of the Gentiles.

   + Jerusalem is a city that dwarfs all other cities in its importance. There is none in the elected purpose and economy of God that can even begin to approach it.

   + God placed Israel in the center of all nations. Three great continents center in that country: Africa, Asia, and Europe. It is a land-bridge between those three great land masses of the earth.

   + The strategic area is also the dividing of time. What happened there divides the centuries. Before the crucifixion of our Lord in that place it is B.C.; after the crucifixion of our Lord in that place, it is A.D.

3. Daniel's Seventy Weeks

   + A tremendous indication of God's purposes in the earth is the time element that is written in this text. Not only is a particular place designated (Jerusalem), but there is also a definite pointing to a certain time: *"And the holy city shall they tread under foot forty and two months"* (11:2).

- Forty-two months. Then, in the next verse, you read, *"And I will give power unto my two witnesses, and they shall prophesy a thousand two hundred and threescore days [forty-two months]"* (11:3).

- More references to this same amount of time can be found in Revelation chapters 12 and 13.

- God did not conjure up that period of time meaninglessly. It is plain what that time period refers, for there, in Daniel, we find those same expressions and those same time frames. By reading Daniel and the apocalypse, it can be seen exactly what it is that God has given to John as He delineates the future of the consummation of the age.

- For instance, in Daniel 9:24, we read, *"seventy weeks."* In the Revised Standard Version, it is translated, *"weeks of years,"* which is correct. In the Hebrew, the word means "weeks of years." The passage reads, *"Seventy sevens [490 years] are determined upon thy people and upon thy holy city, to finish the transgression, and to make an end of sins, and to make reconciliation for iniquity, and to bring in everlasting righteousness, and to seal up the vision and prophecy."*

- Seventy sevens, 490 years, are determined to make an end of sin, to make an end of transgression, and to bring in everlasting righteousness, to seal up the visions and the prophecies, to bring them all to pass.

- The prophet takes those seventy sevens and divides them into two parts. *"Know therefore and understand, that from the going forth of the commandment to restore and to build Jerusalem"* (Daniel 9:25). The decree was issued in Daniel in the twentieth year of Artaxerxes in 445 B.C. Thus, from that day: *"From the going forth of the commandment to restore and to build Jerusalem unto Messiah the Prince [until the coming of Jesus] shall be seven weeks, and threescore and two weeks [sixty-nine weeks].… And after threescore and two weeks shall Messiah be cut off"* (Daniel 9:25–26).

- So, starting at the twentieth year of Artaxerxes and reading forward 483 years, sixty-nine 7s, we come to A.D. 38, when Jesus was cut off, when the Messiah was cut off or put to death.

- Then the prophet separates that last week, that seventieth week. That week is the climax, for that seventieth week brings in the everlasting kingdom of God.

- This is what is referred to in the seventieth week: *"He [the antichrist, the one who wars against God] shall confirm the covenant with many for one week: and in the midst of the week [he is talking to Daniel about Daniel's people, the Jews], he shall cause the sacrifice and the oblation to cease"* (Daniel 9:27).

- Then follows the terrible prophecy here of the great tribulation. So Daniel divides that final week into two parts: the first part into three-and-a-half years and the second part three-and-a-half years—each part, forty-two months, 1,260 days, time, time, and dividing of time, time, times and half time.

- For example, in Daniel 7:25: *"A time and times and the dividing of time."* In Daniel 12:7: *"And swear by him that liveth for ever that it shall be for a time, times, and a half."* The source of that number comes from Daniel's seventieth week, which God divided into three-and-a-half years.

- Between those sixty-nine weeks, at the end of which the Lord is cut off, and this seventieth week that brings in the consummation, there is a great interlude, a great intermission.

- In Ephesians 3, Paul says this great intermission is the time period in which we now live. That great interlude in which we live is a mystery, which is a secret hid in the heart of God.

- God revealed it to His holy apostles that we might rejoice in our election to the household of faith and in our part in the consummation of the age.

4. The Measuring of the Temple (verses 1–2).

- In this chapter, as I have indicated, we are manifestly and openly on Jewish ground.

- Between that sixty-ninth and seventieth week is our present, vast interlude, which we call the "age of grace," the church.

- This tribulation is in two parts: the first part is called "the tribulation" and the second part is called "the great tribulation," each being three-and-a-half years. Then, we know we are looking at Daniel's seventieth week.

- You will find a chapter division between chapters 10 and 11, but it is all a part of the same prophecy.

- The bitterness that lies ahead, dark and tragic, is described in the first verse: *"And there was given to me a reed like unto a rod: and the angel stood, saying, Rise, and measure the temple of God, and the altar, and them that worship therein"* (11:1).

5. What Temple Are We Talking About?

- What is this temple of God? There are five temples in the Bible: 1. Solomon's temple, destroyed by Nebuchadnezzar in 587 B.C.; 2. Zerubbabel's temple, built after the captivity and desecrated by Antichus Ephiphanes in 168 B.C.; 3. Herod's temple, rebuilt in splendor and destroyed by Titus in A.D. 70; 4. the temple we are discussing in this lesson; 5. the millennial temple, described in a prophecy in Ezekiel 40–42.

- For this lesson, we are concerned with the fourth temple. John is commanded to *"Rise, and measure the temple of God, and the altar, and them that worship therein"* (11:1).

- This is the same temple referred to in Daniel, when *"the prince"* (Daniel 9:26), that man of sin, that ultimate antichrist, makes a covenant with the Jewish people, and Israel rebuilds the city and the temple.

- In the middle of that covenant—in the middle of the seventieth week—the terrible prince breaks his promise and even those who befriended Israel turn their vengeance upon the city. It is trampled down for forty-two months—the great tribulation.

- It is the same temple that Paul refers to in 2 Thessalonians 2:4, when he talks about the man of sin *"who opposeth and exhalteth himself above all that is called God, or that is worshipped; so that he as God sitteth in the temple of God, shewing himself that he is God."*

- In Romans 9–11, it is foretold that the Jew will return to Palestine, and God says that the temple will be rebuilt. In his rejection of Christ, in his unbelief, and in the rebuilding of that temple, the Jewish nation shall make friends with the political ruler of the world, which is the great ultimate man of sin.

- But that supposed friend is to reveal his true self in the middle of the week—the middle of the seventieth week, when he shall break his covenant and when the Jewish people are to be trampled underfoot for three-and-a-half years.

- This is a part of the bitterness that John felt in chapter 10 when he took the inheritance, the title deed, which at first tasted like honey, precious like heaven itself, and then, as he looked upon his people crushed in blood, in tears, and in death, the vision because bitter.

- *"There was given to me a reed like unto a rod"* (11:1). Wherever the word *"rod"* is used in Revelation, it refers to chastisement, correction, or judgment. With that rod, John was commanded to measure the temple and the people.

- Many times in the Bible you will find a "measuring" commanded of God. To measure something was also a way to claim it for God. The measurement in Revelation 11 concerns the people of God who are to be measured for judgment and correction.

- When the Jew turns his face toward the homeland and rebuilds his city, Jerusalem, and when he rebuilds the temple and reinstitutes the Mosaic institutions and rituals, he does so with great hope and anticipation.

- But John, in his vision, saw beyond those days of gladness. John saw the rod of the anger of God caused by their unbelief, rejection, and blasphemy against Christ.

- To sum up the first two verses, I would have to say it like this: John was told to measure the temple and the altar (the altar of incense) and to measure the worshippers.

- These worshippers are the faithful, believing Jews of the tribulation days. The temple is the one that shall be built in Jerusalem during the tribulation, the one where ancient Jewish rites will be reinstituted. It is the same temple in which the man of sin will seat himself, demanding to be worshipped.

- The measuring itself is an act of claiming or judgment.

- The outer court is not to be measured. Instead, John is told to cast it out or leave it out. The language indicates utter rejection and the reason is given in verse 2: *"The Gentiles:...shall they tread under foot forty and two months."*

6. The Two Witnesses (verses 3–11)

- The time limit of the mystery of the two witnesses is stated explicitly as 1,260 days.

- Notice that the witnesses are described by a mighty angel because John does not see them.

- We can gather that the time period in which they lived was an unusual age, especially when you consider the fact that if these two witnesses of God were antagonized or if someone desired to hurt them *"fire proceedeth out of their mouth, and devoureth their enemies"* (11:5).

- This is as it was in the days of the old theocracy, when Jereboam built his golden idol calf at Bethel. There came from Judah an unnamed prophet of God who denounced the idolatry and, as he was denouncing it, King Jereboam put forth his right hand to seize the prophet. When he did so, his right hand withered and he could not draw it back. This eleventh chapter of Revelation describes that kind of world, an age and dispensation in which these two witnesses represent God.

7. The Identification of the Two Witnesses

- These men are described in verse 4 as *"two olive trees"* and *"two candlesticks."*

- The figure of olive trees comes from Zachariah 4:3, 14, and it means they are anointed.

- The figure of two candlesticks may also be from the same passage (in which only one lampstand is mentioned) but it evidently refers to the witnesses' character as light-bearers of the truth of God.

- In verses 5 and 6, we see what they do. The conduct of their ministry is spectacular, to say the least. They have power to kill their enemies with fire, to keep it from raining, to turn the waters to blood, and to bring plagues upon the earth. The first two powers remind us of Elijah (see 1 Kings 17) and the last two of Moses (see Exodus 7).

- Therefore, they are, I believe, Elijah and Moses. I believe this is what Scripture is indicating; however, there are many opinions as to who these men are.

8. The True Identify of the Two Witnesses

- I have stated that I think the two witnesses in Revelation 11:3–12 are Elijah and Moses. Here are reasons why I think this to be true:

  a. In Malachi 4:5–6, God's last words in the Old Testament mention the coming of Elijah, and this is clearly a prediction of the Lord: *"Behold, I will send you Elijah the prophet before the coming of the great and dreadful day of the LORD: and he shall turn the heart of the fathers to their children, and the heart of the children to their fathers, lest I come and smite the earth with a curse."* The great and dreadful day of the Lord refers specifically to the latter part of the tribulation period.

  b. Another reason I think these two happen to be Moses and Elijah is the fact that among all the prophets of the Old Testament, two were removed from this world before their ministries were finished: Moses and Elijah.

    - Moses was removed prematurely because he disobeyed God at the rock that provided water. Instead of speaking to the rock in a controlled voice, he shouted at the people and pounded the rock twice with his staff. God graciously sent the water gushing out anyway, but he had some things to say to Moses.

- *"Because ye believe me not, to sanctify me in the eyes of the children of Israel, therefore ye shall not bring this congregation into the land which I have given them"* (Numbers 20:12).

- Moses never set foot in the Promised Land; however, God did allow him to take a good look at the land from the vantage point of Mount Nebo. So Moses died with his ministry unfinished.

- Elijah was a great Old Testament prophet, too—one of the greatest of his time. He took on the four hundred leaders of Baal worship and challenged them to a showdown. God answered Elijah with fire and overwhelmed the worshippers of Baal.

- On Elijah's way back to the capital city, he received a message from the heathen queen, Jezebel. The message claimed that Elijah would be murdered within twenty-four hours. The once courageous prophet ran for his life into the wilderness and asked God to kill him. When God asked Elijah why he wanted to die, he responded with a "woe is me; I am being persecuted"-type of answer.

- God repeated His question and Elijah repeated his pessimistic answer. So God told Elijah, *"Elisha…shalt thou anoint to be prophet in thy room"* (1 Kings 19:16).

- A short time later, God took Elijah to heaven in a whirlwind and a chariot of fire. So Elijah's ministry wasn't finished either.

- But in the coming of the tribulation, Moses and Elijah will get a chance to finish their ministries. The same Moses who couldn't set foot in the Promised Land will preach in the middle of Jerusalem. The same Elijah who ran from Jezebel will shake his fist under the nose of the beast, or the antichrist.

9. What Elijah and Moses Represent

- First of all, as they stand to speak, to witness, and to testify or prophesy, they are clothed in sackcloth. Sackcloth is a heavy, course garment woven out of camel's hair or mohair. It was worn by the ancients as a sign of sorrow and great mourning.

- You will note that, in verse 7, the beast that emerges out of the bottomless pit shall make war against them and shall overcome and kill them. They were protected by the Lord God as long as it was in His will. Even in the days of the terrible beast, these alone in the earth were invincible to harm until their testimony finished. Then they laid down their lives.

- When the beast slew the two witnesses, he suffered not their bodies to be buried. The whole earth looked upon their corpses for three-and-a-half days. A corpse decomposes quickly in a tropical climate. Can you imagine the indescribable shame as these two mighty prophets of God lay in the streets of the great city of Jerusalem and turned to corruption and decay?

- In verse 10, the people rejoice over the death of these two prophets of the Lord God and they send gifts to one another. But God always takes care of His own, and so, in verses 11 and 12, we find that the Lord God looks down from heaven and sees the rejoicing of that evil world over the slaughter of His two witnesses. The Lord breathes life into their decaying bodies and they stand on their feet, *"and their enemies beheld them"* (11:12).

- These same enemies also heard the voice from heaven saying, *"Come up hither"* (11:12). They watch the witnesses ascend into glory in the cloud, in the Shekinah brilliance and burning of the presence of the almighty God.

- There is, in that scene, a pattern that runs throughout the Word of God: *"Every eye shall see him, and they also which pierced him"* (Revelation 1:7).

10. The Ending of the Second Woe (verses 13–14)

  ◆ As God told His servants, Moses and Elijah, to *"Come up hither,"* we read in verse 13, *"And the same hour was there a great earthquake, and the tenth part of the city fell, and in the earthquake were slain of men seven thousand: and the remnant were affrighted, and gave glory to the God of heaven."*

  ◆ In that terrible earthquake judgment, seven thousand men of distinction were slain. Seven thousand of the most prominent men were trying to flee when God shook the earth from center to circumference and they were killed.

  ◆ That same verse says that in that awful hour of judgment, men gave glory to the God of heaven because they were afraid. In their fears, and in their terror, they gave glory to the God of heaven—but at a distance, out of fear, not out of conversion.

  ◆ In verse 13, first, the seven thousand are slain and then, those that remain, called *"the remnant,"* gave glory to the God of heaven.

  ◆ This is the end of the second woe, because, as we read in verse 14, *"the second woe is past; and, behold, the third woe cometh quickly."*

11. The Third Woe Begins

  a. The parenthetical portion between the sixth and seventh trumpets is now concluded.

    ◆ With the sounding of the seventh trumpet comes an announcement that begins in verse 15. Look up this verse:

    _____

    _____

    _____

    _____

    _____

    _____

    ◆ We are entering here the final agony of the earth—its travail, its pain, its suffering, and its judgment in the hands of a furious and wrathful God.

    ◆ There is, here in this world, a kingdom, and it is presided over by the prince of the power of the air and by the powers of darkness. But God declares that sin will not rule in this earth forever. Satan's reign will not remain unchallenged.

  b. A glorious and triumphant scene

    ◆ In verse 16, we see the response of the twenty-four elders. These four and twenty represent God's resurrected, immortalized, raptured, transfigured saints in heaven.

    ◆ The four and twenty elders fell on their faces and worshipped God.

    ◆ In the following verse, we hear their prayer of thanksgiving.

  c. A time of reward

    ◆ In verse 18, we find those who become believers during the tribulation will be resurrected and rewarded at the end of this terrible holocaust—when Jesus returns to earth as King of Kings.

    ◆ The church-age believers—those of us who believed from the day of Pentecost until the rapture of the church—will already be in their new immortal bodies and will have received their reward at the judgment seat of Christ soon after the rapture.

  d. The heavenly temple opened

- In Hebrews, a point is made concerning God's instructions to build everything in the earthly tabernacle according to the exact pattern of the heavenly temple. (See Hebrews 8:5.)

- Evidently, there is a complete temple in heaven, of which the earthly one was only a replica.

- In this verse, we see this heavenly temple opened, revealing the ark of God's covenant.

- The ark was the main piece of furniture in the Holy of Holies of the tabernacle in the wilderness, as well as in the temple in Jerusalem. It had a golden throne on top, the place where the blood of the lamb was sprinkled on the Day of Atonement.

- When this was done, symbolically, this throne changed from a throne of judgment to a throne of mercy. It was called "the mercy seat." It was here that God met man's needs for forgiveness in the Old Testament. Every believing Jew knew that the ark was where God dealt with their national and personal problem of sin and separation from Him.

- The fact that God opens heaven's temple and shows the Jews the ark is to remind them that He will be unconditionally faithful to His covenant of forgiveness, which He makes with those who will accept the message of the Messiah.

- The chapter closes with flashes of lightening and violent thunder—a warning to those who reject the Messiah that the final judgments of God are on their way.

- Here, just before the outpouring of that final judgment of the vials of God, there is a reminder of God's faithfulness to His people—the ark in the temple.

## How Much Do You Remember?

1. In what city does chapter 11 take place?
2. Describe the timeframe delineated in Daniel concerning the seventy weeks.
3. What was John commanded to measure? With what instrument was he to measure with and what does this instrument symbolize?
4. Who can we suppose the two witnesses are? What reasons support this conclusion?
5. With what natural force does the second woe conclude?
6. The third woe begins with a great announcement. How did the twenty-four elders respond?
7. What is the image if the ark of the covenant a reminder of for the Jews?

## Your Assignment for Next Week:

1. Read Revelation chapter 12.
2. Review your notes from this lesson.
3. Underline your Bible.

## Lesson 13 Notes

_____

_____

_____

_____

_____

_____

_____

_____

_____

_____

_____

_____

_____

_____

_____

_____

_____

_____

_____

_____

# Lesson 14
# REVELATION 12

## The Radiant Woman and the War in Heaven

This passage represents a great division in the apocalypse. The first eleven chapters conclude with the sounding of the seventh trumpet, as the kingdoms of this world become the kingdom of our Lord and of His Christ.

In the days of the voice of the seventh trumpet, the mystery of God is revealed and is coming to a finish. Therefore, the Lord gives us a preview, a prophetic outline, of the final days of this present world. In the precise middle of the apocalypse, the Lord begins a delineation of the details, filling in the great, broad, prophetic preview of what is yet to come.

In Revelation 12, we are introduced to some of the persons who are to figure so largely in these last days of God's purpose upon the earth. In this passage in Revelation 12, five personages are introduced in this order:

- First, the woman clothed with the sun—the radiant woman.
- Second, the great red dragon.
- Third, the Man child.
- Fourth, Michael.
- Fifth, the remnant of the seed of women.

1. The Identification of the Radiant Woman

- Look up Revelation 12:1 for the description of this radiant woman:

_____

_____

_____

_____

- There have been many identifications of this woman, with most people identifying her as the Virgin Mary. But I feel that the identification of this radiant woman with the human mother of Jesus is impossible.

- Look at verse 6: "*And the woman fled into the wilderness, where she hath a place prepared of God, that they should feed her there a thousand two hundred and threescore days.*"

- And verse 14: "*And to the woman were given two wings of a great eagle, that she might fly into the wilderness, into her place, where she is nourished for a time, and times, and half a time (three-and-a-half years).*"

- Then, verse 17: "*And to the woman were given two wings of a great eagle, that she might fly into the wilderness, into her place, where she is nourished for a time, and times, and half a time.*"

- These verses separate her from Mary. There are others who say that this radiant woman represents the church. When they do that, they reverse the apocalyptic vision recorded in chapter 12. To say that the church gave birth to Jesus is to be diametrically opposed to Scripture. It is Christ who gave birth to the church; the church is taken out of the side of Christ. We are born out of His flesh, His blood, and His bones.

- Who then is this radiant woman? I believe she is plainly identified in all of the Holy Scriptures. In Romans 9:4–5, Paul describes the *"Who are Israelites; to whom pertaineth the adoption, and the glory, and the covenants, and the giving of the law, and the service of God, and the promises; whose are the fathers, and of whom as concerning the flesh Christ came, who is over all, God blessed for ever."*

- The inspired apostle says that the one who gave birth to the Messiah is the nation and the family and the people of Israel. It is Israel who produced Christ. The nation is likened unto a woman who bore in her womb the great Savior of the world. Christ is the fruit of the womb of Israel.

- When you thus interpret the passage, everything in the Bible will marvelously fit together. Israel is called the married woman, again and again. Israel is referred to as the mother, again and again. Israel is referred to as a widow and as a divorced woman. (See Isaiah 47:7, 9; Isaiah 50:1.)

- Always, the church is referred to as a chaste virgin, a bride who is someday to be presented to Christ.

- Israel always is a mother, giving birth to children. Through Zion's travail, children are born unto God. But the church, the bride of Christ, is unmarried until the great marriage supper of the Lamb.

- So this woman, a mother, giving birth to the Messiah, refers to the nation Israel.

2. The Chronology of the Prophecies of God

- In verse 6, there is a note that tells the whole story and meaning of this revelation: *"And the woman fled into the wilderness, where she hath a place prepared of God, that they should feed her there a thousand two hundred and threescore days."*

- Then again, in verse 14, we find that same indication. Over and over again, we find that same time period mentioned.

- So the chronology, or the source of that period of time, is Daniel's seventieth week divided in two, which gives us three-and-a-half years, 1,260 days, 42 months, or *"a time, and times, and half a time."*

- This is the last prophetic week. At its end, God will bring in the kingdom and the great consummation of the age shall come about.

- Therefore, when we turn to this book of Revelation and read of this woman fleeing into the wilderness, where God cares for her for three-and-a-half years, we immediately know the period described.

- We have come to the great and final end time of this world. This is also called *"the time of Jacob's trouble"* (Jeremiah 30:7).

- Don't forget that in this prophecy of Daniel's seventieth week, and in those periods of time mentioned in Revelation, all of this vast period of time in which we live, the age of grace, is left out.

- In verses 5–6 of this chapter, we find this great gap of time that we call "the period of grace in which we now live." Look up verse 5, and look at the time indicated:

_____

_____

_____

_____

- Just reading this, one would think that Christ had no life at all. One might think He never lived at all, that He was born a child and was caught up to the throne immediately.

- His ministry is not referred to, His life is not referred to, nor His death. But God is not interested in time, and so, in His recording here by John, He is not presenting the chronological life of Christ in order.

3. War in Heaven (verses 7–11)

    a.   Two "wonders" or signs

- Chapter 12 is actually a description of three different scenes: first, there is war on earth (verses 1–6); then a war in heaven (verses 7–12); and finally, another war on earth (verses 13–17).

- In this chapter, you will find two "wonders" introduced. These two wonders are sometimes translated as *"signs,"* indicating an object with special meaning.

- The first sign that we saw was the woman in verses 1–2. We know that this sign, or wonder, was a woman—Israel.

- The second sign is a dragon, found in verses 3–4. The identification of the sign is made in verse 9. The dragon is Satan, but his description in these verses is startling. The use of a dragon to picture Satan indicates intense cruelty.

- In verse 3, the adjective *"red"* indicates its murderous, bloodthirsty character. The seven heads and the ten horns relate it to the antichrist—to the beast that we shall see in chapter 13. The crowns on its head indicate regal power. With its tail it is said to draw a third part of the stars of heaven and cast them to the earth.

    b.   Michael and Lucifer

- This war speaks of the violence between Michael and the dragon. It is a war between Michael and his angels and Satan and his angels.

- This conflict is nothing new because it has been going on throughout the ages. Those two have known one another and have faced each other since the beginning of time when God created the heavenly host.

- For example, in the ninth verse of Jude, we have the same two antagonizing each other: *"Yet Michael the archangel, when contending with the devil he disputed about the body of Moses, durst not bring against him a railing accusation, but said, The Lord rebuke thee."* These are the identical participants named here in this final war in heaven.

- Michael and his angels fight against Lucifer and his angels. Lucifer is also called the *"son of the morning"* in Isaiah 14:12. In Ezekiel 28:14, he is described as *"the anointed cherub that covereth,"* which means he was the highest created angel of God—God's highest creation. But in those days before time was born, arrogance filled Lucifer's heart to assume possession of the reins of the universe and of the throne of God itself. Even the strength and power of Michael, the archangel of God, could not stand before the tremendous might and glory of Lucifer.

    c.   The defeat of Satan

- Don't forget that the kingdom of this world cannot and will not become the sovereignty of our Lord and of His Christ until the sounding of the seventh trumpet—and that's where we are in the book of Revelation.

- Notice, in verses 8–9, the result of the battle is defeat for Satan and his host. They are cast out of heaven and into the earth. In verse 9, Satan has five titles: dragon (fierce nature), serpent (crafty character), devil (accuser or slanderer), Satan (adversary), and deceiver of the entire world.

- In verse 12, the voice from heaven announces woe on the inhabitants of the earth because the devil has been barred from heaven and will wage his total warfare on the earth. Now, the only sphere of operation for Lucifer or Satan is upon the earth. He also knows that his time is limited, as you will notice in this verse.

- At this defeat of Satan, a voice in heaven breaks into praise. (See verse 10.) It announces salvation in that kingdom, since one more major conquest has been made in the march toward inevitable victory for Christ.

- You will notice in verse 10 that Satan is called *"the accuser of our brethren."* This reveals something about Satan's work through the years and why he has been victorious throughout this age and in the ageless past. His activity continues day and night before God, thus making it clear that this has been, and is, his work up to the middle of the tribulation, when he will be cast out from heaven.

- Yes, Satan accuses God's people day and night. There has never lived a man who could stand up say, "I am pure in all my thoughts. All these things Satan says about me is wrong. I have been perfect in all my life." When Satan says, "Look at him, how vile and how sinful," we all must bow our head in shame and say, "Yes that is true." But the Bible says, in verse 11, *"And they overcame him by the blood of the Lamb, and by the word of their testimony; and they loved not their lives unto the death."*

4. A Conclusion of Chapter 12 (verses 12–17)

- Notice verse 12: *"Woe to the inhabiters of the earth and of the sea! for the devil is come down unto you, having great wrath, because he knoweth that he hath but a short time."*

- As anticipated, we see in verse 13 that Satan's attack shall be upon the woman—Israel. This was anticipated in verse 6.

- In verse 14, the eagle's wings indicates rapid flight, which will be necessary for Israel to escape the attacks of Satan during this terrible time of great tribulation.

- I personally believe that these people—Israel—will find asylum, which gives them natural protection for time, times, and a half time or three-and-a-half years—the last part of the tribulation. That wilderness refuge will be, I believe, the deserted city of Petra in southern Palestine.

- In verses 15–17, we find that Satan can also work miracles, because he will launch his attack with a flood, apparently, in order to drown people out of their wilderness refuge.

- God, in turn, will cause the earth to open—perhaps another earthquake—in order to consume the water of the flood and, thus, save the persecuted people. When Satan fails to destroy or conquer those who have fled into the wilderness, he turns his attack on *"the remnant of her seed"* (12:17). In other words, when Satan realizes that he has not been successful, he will inspire his followers to hunt and kill anyone and everyone who has believed in Christ. Notice the words in verse 17: *"And the dragon was wroth with the woman,"* which means he was mad at Israel.

- You will read in Romans 11:5, as well as in Revelation 14:1–5, that there is always a remnant who *"keep the commandments of God, and have the testimony of Jesus Christ"* (12:17).

5. A summary of chapter 12

- To summarize chapter 12, we have:
  a. First, the woman, Israel
  b. Second, Satan, or Lucifer
  c. Third, the child, or Christ
  d. Fourth, the archangel, Michael
  e. Fifth, the Jewish remnant

- The other two persons involved we shall see in chapter 13 in our next lesson.

## How Much Do You Remember?

1. Which five personages are introduced in chapter 12?
2. How is the radiant woman described? Who is this woman?
3. What sign is used to represent Satan in verses 3–4? How do the adjectives used relate to Satan's character?
4. Who is the war in heaven between?
5. Why were wings given to the woman in verse 14? What were they symbolic of?

## Your Assignment for Next Week:

1. Read Revelation chapter 13.
2. Review your notes from this lesson.
3. Underline your Bible.

## Lesson 14 Notes

_____

_____

_____

_____

_____

_____

_____

_____

_____

_____

_____

_____

_____

_____

_____

_____

_____

_____

_____

_____

# Lesson 15
# REVELATION 13

## The Antichrist and the False Prophet

1. A Brief Review

   + During the tribulation period, Satan will control a man who will rule the whole world and be known as the antichrist.

   + We saw the first presentation of that man of sin with the opening of the first seal in Revelation 6:2. He does not first appear here in chapter 13, but at the beginning of the opening of the judgments.

   + This antichrist will pretend to be a friend of Israel for the first three-and-a-half years of the tribulation period, but he will then turn on them at the time Satan is cast out of heaven.

   + I believe that this will be the point when Satan personally indwells the antichrist. Since Satan does not have the powers of omnipresence and can only be in one place at a time (and is now confined to the earth by divine decree, as we saw in chapter 12), he makes himself visible by clothing himself with the humanity of the man called the antichrist, or the man of sin.

   + No longer can he enter into the presence of God, for he has been cast out of the heavenlies. In wrath, he comes down to the earth knowing he has but a short time.

   + Revelation 12:12 says, "*Woe to the inhabiters of the earth and of the sea! for the devil is come down unto you, having great wrath, because he knoweth that he hath but a short time.*" We shall find in Revelation 13:5 that the short time is described as forty-two months, three-and-a-half years, or 1,260 days.

2. A Description of this Man of Sin

   + This one described in these first ten verses of Revelation 13 will be the political leader of this world.

   + The one described in the second part of Revelation 13, beginning at verse 11, shall be described as the religious leader of this world and is called the false prophet.

   + A biographical sketch of this man of sin appears in chapter 13, but he is called by various names throughout the Bible. They include "*king of Babylon*" (Isaiah 14:4), "*little horn*" (Daniel 7:8; 8:9), "*the man of sin*" and "*the son of perdition*" (2 Thessalonians 2:3), "*antichrist*" (1 John 2:18), and "*beast*" (Revelation 13:1).

   + He will be a supreme humanist who believes passionately that man can solve his own dilemmas. He will be against everything the Bible teaches and will seem to have a solution for every problem.

3. The Beast from the Raging Sea—The Political Ruler of this World (verses 1–10)

   + The apostle John, you will recall, was "*in the Spirit*"—when he first stood on the Isle of Patmos. Then, he was later taken up into heaven, out into the wilderness, and finally to a high mountain to see visions.

   + Here, in the Spirit, John stands on the shore of a raging sea. That sea is described in Daniel 7. As John stands on the sands of that turbulent and fearful sea, he sees, rising out of it, a monster. As he watches the storm and fury of the raging sea, he sees a beast emerge.

   + The antichrist is called a "*beast*" because that's what he is in the sight of God.

   + Why does the beast emerge from the sea? John explains the figure in Revelation 17:15: "*The waters which thou sawest, where the whore sitteth, are peoples, and multitudes, and nations, and tongues.*" Isaiah put it, "*The wicked are like the troubled sea, when it cannot rest, whose waters cast up mire and dirt*" (Isaiah 57:20).

- So this figure, the beast, rises from the chaos of the troubled world.
  a. A vision of the beast
    - John describes the beast as having ten horns, each wearing a diadem.
    - There appear seven heads supporting those ten horns.
    - Then emerges the whole terrible creature, himself.
    - His body looks like a leopard, his feet like those of a bear, his mouth like that of a lion, his heads have *"the name of blasphemy"* (13:1), and he speaks blasphemy against God, against God's dwelling place, and against those who tabernacle in heaven.
  b. The interpretation of the vision of the beast
    - God has given us, in this vision of the monstrous beast called the antichrist, a symbol of the last political power that shall hold sway in this earth.
    - This is the end of world government. The sovereignty of nations, kingdoms, kings, and rulers of the earth are through.
    - This vision refers back to the book of Daniel. There, in chapter 2, a similar vision is seen, with each body part of the beast representing a political kingdom. Revelation 17 also provides clues for the interpretation of this chapter.
    - In chapter 17, the seven heads are said to be the seven mountains, describing the capital city. The seven heads are also seven kings: *"Five are fallen, and one is, and the other is not yet come"* (Revelation 17:10).
    - Combining information from Daniel 7, Revelation 17, and Revelation 13, I am persuaded that John wrote in that day and in that time, and I believe, as we place ourselves in his position, that the five fallen kings are the five ancient empires that preceded the day of the apostle. The first kingdom was Assyria, with its wild city of Nineveh. The second kingdom was Egypt, with its pyramids and astrological specifications. The third kingdom was the Babylonian Empire of Daniel's day, which perfected the black arts. The fourth was the Medo-Persian Empire that was enslaved by the Babylonians. The fifth kingdom was the Greek Empire, with its idolatrous religions.
    - They are the five fallen ones. But what about the other two? *"And one is"* refers to an existing kingdom in John's day, the Roman Empire. The kingdom that is *"not yet come"* is this great, final, political dominion presided over by the antichrist, which is world government in its ultimate form.
    - Revelation 17:12: *"The ten horns which thou sawest are ten kings, which have received no kingdom as yet."* From John's viewpoint, the ten horns were future kingdoms.
    - The one ultimate apocalyptic government of this world will be divided into ten kingdoms, and *"these have one mind, and shall give their power and strength unto the beast"* (17:13). They will willingly yield their sovereignty and their dominion to this great arch-regent, here described as a beast, who will preside in authority and power over the earth.
    - In Revelation 12:3, we are introduced to Satan, or the dragon: *"And there appeared another wonder* [a sign, a symbol] *in heaven."* That sign or symbol is still being described here in chapter 13, except in human form. This is Satan incarnate, in the flesh. This is the personal rule of Satan upon the earth.
    - From this, then, we must agree that the beast described here is a man—a particular person. This, in chapter 13, is God's delineation of that man. All of these beasts and images describe him.

- We know that he is a man because this is clear in the description of his final overthrow in Revelation 19:20, which says, *"And the beast was taken, and with him the false prophet…. These both were cast alive into a lake of fire burning with brimstone."*
- There can only be one leader of this final world government. Here is a description of a man, and that man is the ultimate antichrist.
- One of the most remarkable statements in all of the Word of God is written by this same apostle in 1 John 2:18, where he says, *"Little children…ye have heard that antichrist shall come…."*
- They heard that the antichrist was to come because all of the teaching and testimony of the Word of God spoke of that coming. That common doctrine or revelation—wherever the Word of God was preached—was a part of every framework of the holy revelation of God, clearly teaching that there was to be the arrival of an ultimate and final antichrist.

4. His Personal Attractiveness (verses 4–5)

- This man shall be a fascinating, intriguing, personal power. He will be one of the most magnetic mortal men that ever walked across the stage of human history.
- Revelation 13:2–4, *"And the dragon [Satan] gave him his power, and his seat, and great authority…. And all the whole world wondered after the beast, and they worshipped the dragon which gave power unto the beast: and they worshipped the beast, saying, Who is like unto the beast? who is able to make war with him?"*
- Satan gives the antichrist his power, his throne, and his authority. Therefore, this man accepts the gift that Jesus spurned when Satan offered Him the same thing—all the kingdoms of this world. (See Matthew 4:1–11.) Now the antichrist accepts that same gift and the whole earth acclaims him as the very incarnation of glory, wisdom, might, power, and honor.
- This man of sin will be received with gladness and the kings of the earth will yield their authority to him, for *"who is like unto the beast?"*
- Out of the chaos and violence of human history there always arises one of these leaders. Out of the chaos and blood of the French Revolution came Napoleon; out of the chaotic revolution of the labor movement came Lenin; out of the chaos and terrible revolution of the thirties came Hitler. Always, out of the roiling turmoil of social chaos, there comes an antichrist. So it is with this one.
- When we saw him in chapter 6. He was riding on a white horse, coming to conquer. In the midst of this chaos and despair, the kings and rulers of the earth gladly yield to him the authority and dominion of the governments of the world. They hail him as savior of the race.
- I think we are living in a time when such a man—in God's timing—could rise upon the scene. Never in the history of this world has there been ten nations that could be called "a revived Roman Empire," which the prophet Daniel called *"a kingdom, which shall never be destroyed"* (Daniel 2:24), or the *"one is"* of John's time. But now we see such a thing happening.

5. He Will Have Miraculous Power

- The antichrist will be able to fool people into thinking that his miraculous power is real.
- You will notice that they begin to worship him after a miracle occurs in verses 3-4, *"And I saw one of his heads as it were wounded to death; and his deadly wound was healed…. And they worshipped the dragon which gave power unto the beast."*
- This indicates that Satan will have miraculous powers to heal.

6. The Book of Life

- In verse 8, John speaks of a book called *"the book of life of the Lamb slain from the foundation of the world."*

+ The ones whose names are not written in that book will worship the antichrist.

+ Satan will be furious with those whose names are in the book of life because they trusted in Christ.

7. God's Encouragement (verses 9–10)

   + God closes this passage with the statement, *"If any man have an ear, let him hear"* (13:9).

   + This expression is found many times in the Word of the Lord. We find it in Matthew, Luke, and seven times in Revelation 2 and 3, each time the Lord speaks to one of the churches. But notice the difference here.

   + In chapters 2 and 3, he said, *"He that hath an ear, let him hear what the Spirit saith unto the churches."* This is the Word of the Lord seven times, but we do not have that last phrase here.

   + We only have the statement, *"If a man have an ear, let him hear."* We do not have the last phrase, which says, *"what the Spirit saith unto the churches."*

   + This is because the church is gone; they were taken out of this world before the tribulation. But to the saints who turn to God in this fearful and bloody hour, He says, *"If any man have an ear, let him hear."*

   + By one means or another, all over the world, believers will have to suffer under the hands of this satanic creature called the antichrist. Hear the final words in this portion of Scripture: *"Here is the patience and the faith of the saints"* (13:10). God is not forgetful of trials suffered in His name. The Lord limits the extent of the persecution—here it is forty-two months.

   + In the permissive will of God, every tyrant, every antichrist that has ever appeared on the scene, or that shall appear, endures only according to the permissive will of God. As we read in verse 10, *"He that leadeth into captivity shall go into captivity: he that killeth with the sword must be killed with the sword."*

   + This is a picture of the antichrist. Now we study his cohort, the religious leader framed and pictured for us in the second half of this chapter.

8. The Vile False Prophet (verses 11–18)

   a. The second beast

      + The first ten verses of Revelation 13 describe the political and ultimate antichrist. Now, beginning in verse 11, John describes the false prophet in one of the most instructive of all the visions to be found in the apocalypse.

      + This chapter begins with the description of a beast that comes out of the raging sea.

      + This second beast arises from the earth and in chapters 16, 19, and 20. He is called "the false prophet."

      + He looks like a lamb, he has two horns like a little lamb, but when he speaks, his voice betrays him, for he has the voice of a dragon and the heart of a serpent.

      + He exercises authority and military power in the name of the antichrist. He does miraculous things as he uses the power of the state to coerce the whole world to bow down and conform to his program and to the will of the first beast—the antichrist.

   b. Contrasting the first and second beast

      + The first beast rises out of the sea; the second beast rises out of the earth. In the turmoil, strife, and raging conflict of races, nations, and economic orders, this ultimate antichrist rises to preside over the might and strength of the whole world. All dictators arise out of social disruption. This second beast arises out of the land—out of the earth. He comes out of an established civil order. He does not come out of chaos, as the first beast does, but, rather, he is a product of an ordered society.

- The first beast is political; the second beast is religious. The first beast is crowned as king and as a military ruler over the world. This second beast is like a lamb, exercising power to deceive the whole world into accepting the authority, program, and the self-chosen deity of the antichrist. As this antichrist builds a kingdom for himself through the yielded sovereignty of the ten kings, he has, by his side, a partner—the false prophet.

- The first beast and the second beast help and support one another. This is unusual because, in the kingdom of evil, you will find the leaders destroying one another. Such is the kingdom of darkness and evil, tearing itself apart. That is why this is such an astonishing prophecy here in Revelation. These two act like blood brothers. One gives authority, financial support, and political power to the other, and the other takes it and uses it for the tremendous, unbelievable, immeasurable support of the first.

9. The Lamb-Like False Prophet

- The appearance of the false prophet is very different from the first beast, and less pretentious.

- He has two horns (instead of ten), like a lamb. What could be more sweet or tender than someone who counsels people, who seeks to make them conscious of God, who ensures their happiness and solves all their problems?

- This fellow, the false prophet, has a "softness" about him that is deceiving. Of the two—he is far more dangerous, because any man who proposes to guide and command the consciences, minds, hearts, and souls of men has in his power an unbelievable authority over mankind.

- From this description, we know that he is a product of an apostate and perverted Christianity.

- A second remarkable thing about him is that he imitates all of the things that are of the Lord. For instance, Paul said, *"I bear in my body the marks* [stigmata] *of the Lord Jesus"* (Galatians 6:17). In Revelation 7, we find those stigmata, the markings or seal of God, upon Israel. In chapter 14, we find them again upon the 144,000. We find them upon God's saints in heaven—the mark of Christ, the mark of God. But this fellow, the false prophet, has a mark that he places on the hand and on the forehead of all of his followers.

- Another amazing thing about him is that he is able to perform miracles.

- The most astonishing development is the use by the false prophet of his authority and power to promote idolatrous worship.

- The false prophet—the one like a lamb—will try to duplicate the Christian church and convince it to follow him. It will be this unbelievable idolatry that shall come to pass during the days of the antichrist.

- You may recall that the first great world kingdom was represented by a tremendous image. That first world empire was the golden sovereignty of Nebuchadnezzar. (See Daniel 3:1.) He sent out a decree that all must bow down before his god of gold. When we turn to the last kingdom of the age, humanity repeats that same weakness.

- Revelation 13:14–17 describes the terrible mandate of the false prophet. There is an idolatrous program to follow and an image to adore, and if one does not obey, he or she is violently coerced by a political, financial, and military authority given to this false prophet.

10. The Amazing Number 666 (verse 18)

- The false prophet says, *"Here is wisdom. Let him that hath understanding count the number of the beast: for it is the number of a man; and his number is Six hundred three score and six* [666]*"* (3:18). That is the most infamous of all of the apocalyptic figures in history and in literature.

- Although there are a thousand speculations about what this means, there is one thing we know: six is the number of a man. The number six means falling short of perfection. Man was created on the sixth day. He is to work six of the seven days. A Hebrew slave could not be a slave more than six years. The fields were not to be sown more than six years and were then allowed to be fallow—given a Sabbath rest.

+ There is a trinity of sixes here. The beast, in his number, represents the penultimate of all human ingenuity. The most mankind will be able to attain shall be under and below perfection—seven. He himself is a six, his national government is a six, and the whole program by which he seeks to make one world religion is that discouraging six.

+ Had the apocalypse closed with the thirteenth chapter, our lives would be most discouraging and full of despair. But as we turn the pages beyond in this prophecy, we find perfection.

+ Here is the perfect Holy Spirit, the seven spirits of God. Beyond is the holy, blessed, next world, the blessing that God has poured out upon His new creation. Only the Christian will know perfection—and our factory, our ultimate and final government and our marvelous salvation, shall be in the hands of the Lamb of God. Those of us who claim the name of Christ shall not have the mark of the beast.

11. A Brief Review of the False Prophet

+ Here are the things that we ought to remember about this false prophet:

    a. He exercises unlimited authority—verse 12.

    b. He forces people to worship the antichrist—verse 12.

    c. He performs great miracles—verse 13.

    d. He deceives the population—verse 14.

    e. He forces people to worship the image of the antichrist in the temple—verse 14.

    f. He murders all who will not conform—verse 15.

    g. He forces people to receive the mark of the beast—verse 16.

+ When you look at verse 14, you find that he causes people to make an image of the beast. Then, in verse 15, he has the power to give life unto the image of the beast. I believe that this image will be erected in the middle of the reconstructed temple.

+ What will happen to the millions of people who agree to the false prophet's threats and receive the mark of the beast? The Scripture tells us in Revelation 14:9–10:

> *If any man worship the beast and his image and receive his mark in his forehead, or in his hand, the same shall drink of the wine of the wrath of God, which is poured out without mixture into the cup of his indignation; and he shall be tormented with fire and brimstone in the presence of the holy angels, and in the presence of the Lamb.*

+ The title of "antichrist" is one that has been discussed throughout history. Some people think that this second beast is the antichrist, because he has to do, chiefly, with religious matters, while the first beast is principally concerned with political activities.

+ The first beast is obviously a religious leader in one instance: it is he who will be worshipped, not the second beast. It seems to me that the label "antichrist" is to be used for the most important personage, and that, of course, is the first beast.

+ In my mind, the first beast is the antichrist, the man of sins (see 2 Thessalonians 2:3), the little horn (see Daniel 7:8), the prince that shall come (see Daniel 9:26), and the beast (see, for example, Revelation 11:7; 14:9).

+ We come next to the study of that blessed 144,000 with the Lamb on Mt. Zion, and that shall be another interlude.

## How Much Do You Remember?

1. How will the man of sin and the false prophet each lead the world?
2. What does John see emerging from the raging sea? What does the raging sea represent?
3. How is the first beast described and how can that vision be interpreted?
4. Describe the man of sin. How will he be received and what abilities will he have?
5. Out of what does the false prophet arise and what does he appear like?
6. What is the false prophet capable of?
7. What meaning does the number 666 carry?

## Your Assignment for Next Week:

1. Read Revelation chapter 14.
2. Review your notes from this lesson.
3. Underline your Bible.

## Lesson 15 Notes

_____

_____

_____

_____

_____

_____

_____

_____

_____

_____

_____

_____

_____

_____

_____

_____

_____

_____

_____

# Lesson 16
# REVELATION 14

## The 144,000 on Mt. Zion

1. Chapter 14 Is the Counterpart of Chapter 13

   + These two chapters are contemporaneous in history. These things all happen at once.

   + On one side is the dark destruction of the beast, of Satan, and of the judgment of God upon those who worship the image of the beast.

   + At the same time, in contrast, we are given this beautiful scene of these glorious ones who serve God, and Him alone.

2. The Vision

   + The vision opens with John seeing *the* Lamb (not "a" lamb) and 144,000 on Mt. Zion.

   + Mt. Zion is in reference to the heavenly Jerusalem in Hebrews 12:22. Since the 144,000 are before the throne (see verse 3), it seems more natural to understand Zion as the heavenly city.

   + More importantly, the 144,000 are now with the Lamb. When the group was first introduced, they were on earth (see Revelation 7:1–3), but now, they are in heaven.

   + You may wonder if this 144,000 is the same group in chapter 7. Here are some clues that prove this number references the same group:

   a. First, the 144,000 sing their new song in the presence of the elders. So there must be a difference between the elders and the 144,000.

   b. Second is the number itself in the text. That is not the first time we have met the 144,000. We were introduced to that same number in Revelation 7, and here, in chapter 14, the number is presented as though we had met it before. There is nothing about it to distinguish it from the 144,000 that we have met before. The number is so unusual, and the whole situation is so remarkable, that we could suppose the reference in both chapters is the same.

   + Revelation 7:3–4, says, in essence, "Wait until you seal the servants—the ministers of God in their foreheads. And I heard the number of them that were sealed were 144,000." Then John lists twelve thousand that shall come from each tribe of Israel.

   + We must note that all of these people, their separate groups, are together in the same vision. Here are the elders, and over there are the 144,000, sealed of God. Here in the same vision, at the same time, are the great throngs of Gentiles who stand before God and the Lamb, clothed with white robes, out of every kindred, nation, people, tongue, and tribe under the sun. They are all here together.

   + So, seeking to find what God means by these marvelous revelations, let me give you this simple explanation: First, the elders, twenty-four in number, represent the glorified saints of God in the Old and New Testament—the twelve patriarchs and the twelve apostles stand before God.

   + The same symbolism is found in the beautiful city of Jerusalem. There are twelve gates, each one representing one of the twelve patriarchs, one of the twelve tribes of Israel. The city has twelve foundations, each one representing the name of an apostle. The city represents the old and the new, all the saints of God, the old dispensation and the new dispensation. The great multitude coming out of every nation, language, and tribe are those who have been won to Christ by these 144,000 messengers sealed of God.

- In Revelation 14:4, the 144,000 are referred to as the *"firstfruits."* This 144,000 must be the first fruits unto God of this new era, tribe, and period after the translation of the church, after the rapture of the people of God, represented by the elders crowned and enthroned in heaven.

- Before those last days of tribulation begin, God says, in essence, "First, seal for me these 144,000." They are the first ones set aside, called here *"the firstfruits unto God and to the Lamb"* (14:4).

- Then John saw the great multitude of the Gentiles, which no man could number, coming out of the great tribulation wearing robes washed and made white in the blood of the Lamb.

- Thus, these 144,000 are the first fruits unto God in the new beginning, of the time after the days of the Gentiles.

- When our present history has run its course, when the church is done and the age of grace has passed, when God has taken His people out of the earth and we are raptured and translated, then comes this final day described here in the apocalypse.

3. Attributes of the 144,000

  - In chapter 7, we see the 144,000 in their ministry upon the earth. In chapter 14, we see the 144,000 on Mt. Zion with the Lamb. Their task is finished, their work is done, and they are being rewarded by the Lord God for their devoted faithfulness.

  - Note the attributes of these unusual preachers of Christ.

    a. First, during a time when it meant death to have the mark of God and to confess Christ as Lord, these evangelists are preserved from martyrdom by the Spirit of God.

    b. Also, notice their completed number. In chapter 7, God seals 144,000. Here at the end, when they finish their ministry and are numbered before God, they are exactly 144,000—not one has been lost. When we apply this to ourselves, it simply means that when our names are written in the Lamb's book of life, they are there forever. When a man is saved, he is saved forever.

    c. In verse 3, we notice another attribute of this group: they sing a new song that no one else on earth can sing. They are different and have had, at this particular time, a unique and separate ministry. These 144,000 comprise a unique ministry unto the Lord and no one will be able to sing that song except them. This does not mean that anyone else is denied. The elders are there and they are separate and different from the 144,000. These elders are crowned, enthroned, and seated. The 144,000 are not crowned, they are not enthroned, and they are not seated. They are in different orders. The extent of the exaltation of these 144,000 is unknown, but they are not exalted like the elders, nor as you are going to be exalted. Just as everyone is different down here, so we are going to differ up there.

    d. In verse 4, the text says that the 144,000 are virgins and they *"follow the Lamb withersover he goeth."* This is not referring to celibates, but to separation from spiritual fornication and adultery. An example of this is given by Paul in 2 Corinthians 11:2, which says, *"For I have espoused you to one husband, that I may present you as a chaste virgin to Christ."* Likewise, when the text describes these people in Revelation as virgins, it refers to the fact that they have separated themselves from the corruptions of the earth.

    e. In verse 5, we find these words: *"In their mouth was found no guile [lying]: for they are without fault."* That describes God's people. You don't need to have a Christian put his hand on the Bible to swear that what he says is true. When he says a thing, it is so. This verse describes the ultimate sanctification of these people.

4. The Angel Messengers (verses 6–13)

  - There are seven angel messengers who make tremendous announcements regarding the consummation of the age.

a. The first angel messenger (see verse 7) is a preacher, announcing the gospel of the Son of God, and calling men everywhere to repentance.

- In the days of the apocalypse, when the witness of God's servants is drowned in blood, there is still a witness. There is still this angel messenger who stands in the sky and thunders to the ends of the earth the eternal gospel of the Son of God.
- In verse 7, the message that is preached by this angel is threefold—fear God, give glory to Him, and worship Him that made heaven, earth, and the sea.

b. The second angel messenger (verse 8) announces the fall of Babylon.

- This chapter is something like a table of contents for the remainder of the book. The angel announces the fall of Babylon, but the actual description of that fall will be studied in chapters 17 and 18.
- You will note the repetition of the words "is fallen," which emphasizes the certainty of the utter destruction of Babylon, which shall be destroyed because of her own fornication and because she has infected all of the nations of the earth.

c. The third angel messenger (verses 9–11) announces the eternal torment of those who worship and follow the beast.

- Those who worship the beast and his image, and those who receive his mark, shall be punished.
- Notice in verses 10–11 that the punishment described is as terrible as anything that occurs anywhere else in the Bible.
- Notice the words: "The same shall drink of the wine of the wrath of God, which is poured out without mixture into the cup of his indignation; and he shall be tormented with fire and brimstone" (14:10).

d. The fifth messenger announces the reaping of the harvest of the earth (verses 14–16).

- The marvelous message concerning those who die in the Lord is presented to us in verses 12 and 13.
- You will notice that this is not an observation of John, but it is a commandment, a mandate, a decree by God the Father in heaven: "And I heard a voice from heaven saying unto me, Write…" (14:13).
- This is the verdict of God concerning His children who die in the earth, namely, those who are blessed of the Lord.
- These words are written for those who were martyred and perished in that day of awful trial and tribulation, but the comfort, assurance, and strength of it is for all of God's saints in all generations.
- Notice the words: "blessed are the dead which die in the Lord" (14:13). The Bible, without exception, avows the comforting truth that, upon death, immediately, we are blessed; not at some other time, not in some other era, but in the moment of death, the child of God is blessed by being received into the presence of the Lord.
- Notice verse 13: "Yea, saith the Spirit, that they may rest from their labours." Those two words— "rest" and "labours"—describe life in heaven very differently from the popular conception of our day. Most conceive the life to come as sitting on a cloud, but such is not God's portrayal of our eternal life in glory. The revelation of God to us is this: the life that is yet to come is to be filled with intensive activity. There is that heavenly work to be done to the praise and the glory of God that shall never end. The word "rest" does not mean inactivity, but refreshment and rejuvenation. The word "labour" means "weariness" or the fatigue and toil of laborious

activity. When we serve God in the glory that is yet to come, every activity will be with new refreshment.

- The final words of this same verse are: *"and their works do follow them."* Our works do not precede but follow our commitment of faith. This is true throughout the Scripture. The faithful teaching here in Revelation 14 is that preceding us is the grace and love of Jesus: not our works first, but our works last. God says all of the earthly assignments, tasks, and works become an eternal reward for those who fall asleep in Christ. When a man dies, he doesn't die; his works follow him and they are multiplied, one upon the other. Therefore, rewards will not be given until the Lord Jesus says it is time for us to appear before the judgment seat of Christ.

  e. The last two angel messengers announce the battle of Armageddon on the great and final day of the Lord (verses 17–20).

  - The first of these two angel messengers is yielding a sharp sickle.
  - The second angel, who had power over fire, commands the first angel to use his sickle to reap the earth and *"gather the clusters of the vine of the earth"* (4:18) and *"cast it into the great winepress of the wrath of God"* (4:19).

5. The Harvest of the Earth, as Announced by the Angels

- There are two visions here in this section of the Scripture. The first vision is recorded in verses 14–16, the second in verses 17–20.

  a. The first vision is of a harvest. It uses terminology concerning the reaping of wheat.

  - It is personally supervised by the Son of Man, who, as predicted in a parable by Jesus (see Matthew 13:39–43), is careful to gather all of the wheat and keep it separate from the tares. This parable in Matthew explains this first vision.
  - Jesus does not do the dividing himself. Instead, He carefully sees the separation of wheat and tares so that not one believer (wheat) is judged with the tares (unbelievers).
  - This separating work is done by the sixth angel and happens just prior to the Lord's triumphant reappearance to the earth at the end of the tribulation. The day of grace is ended at this point.

  b. The second vision, in verses 17–20, is very different from the first in that the Son of Man doesn't supervise the reaping.

  - This harvest is done by the seventh angel of heaven.
  - This vision has reference to a definite and horrible holocaust that is prophesied through all the Word of God.
  - From the altar, there came an angel who had power over fire.
  - This vision describes the last day of God's permissive will for wickedness and rejection.
  - The vine of the earth is used as a contradistinction to the vine of heaven. The vine of the earth is the vine of rejection, of unbelief, and of unrepentance.
  - Notice that it was the grapes that were cast into the winepress, but when they were ground under the heel of the omnipotent Almighty, blood came out. It was such a flow of blood that it came up to the bridals of the horses and it flowed by the space of a thousand and six hundred furlongs.
  - The word *"furlongs"* is a measurement of an eighth of a mile. So, for two hundred miles, there was a river of blood in this final catastrophe of the day of the Almighty.

- That is the first reference in the book of Revelation to the indescribably awesome, terrible, and final battle called the battle of Armageddon.

## How Much Do You Remember?

1. What is the difference between the 144,000 in chapter 7 and here in chapter 14?
2. Describe the attributes of the 144,000.
3. Review the seven angel messengers. What does each announce?
4. Look at verse 13, namely the words *"rest"* and *"labour."* What is the popular conception about our life to come, and how does God intend that life to be according to His revelation?
5. Describe the two visions of the harvest in verses 14–20. How do they differ?

## Your Assignment for Next Week:

1. Read Revelation chapter 15.
2. Review your notes from this lesson.
3. Underline your Bible.

## Lesson 16 Notes

_____

_____

_____

_____

_____

_____

_____

_____

_____

_____

_____

_____

_____

_____

_____

_____

_____

_____

_____

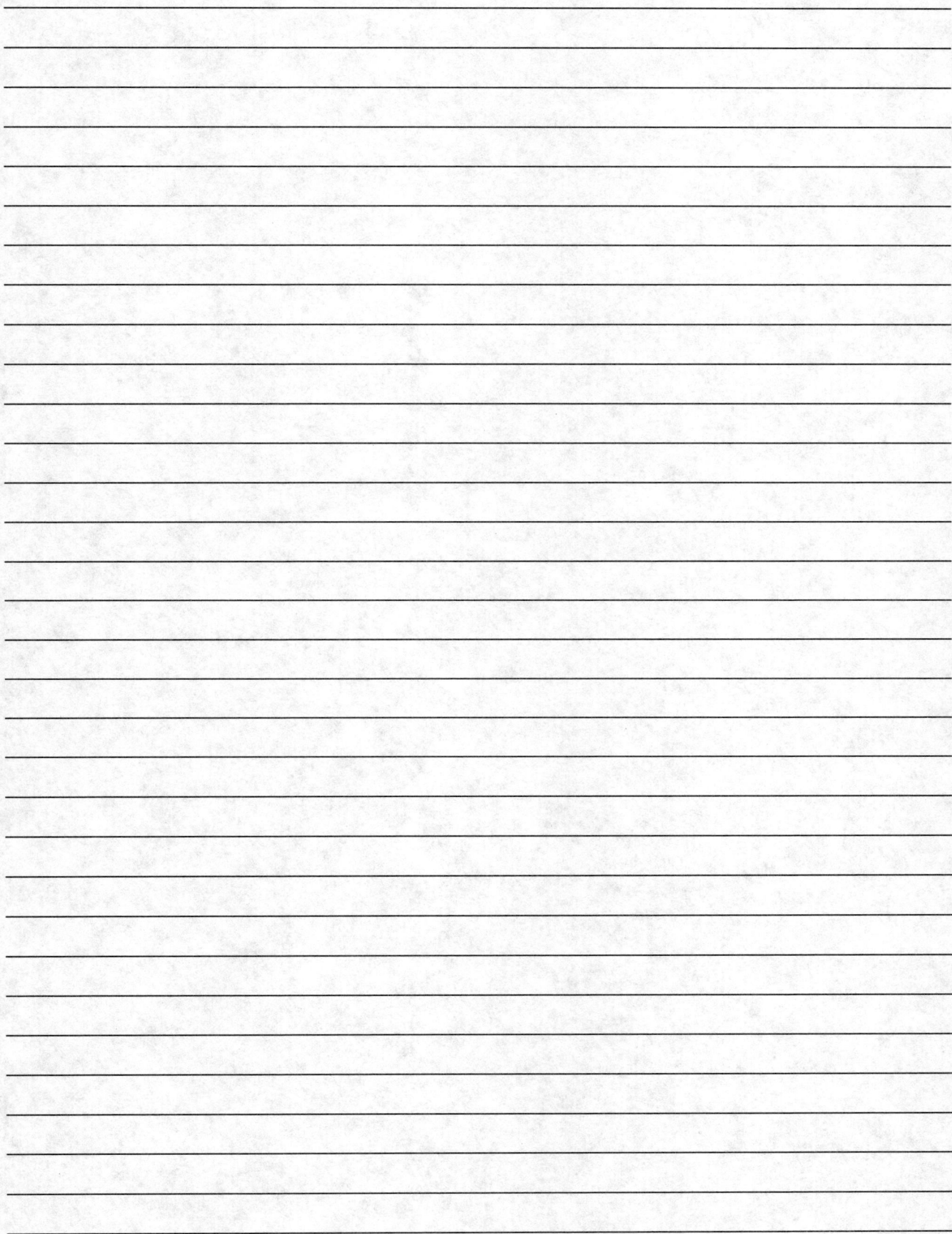

# Lesson 17
# REVELATION 15

1. The Prelude to the Last Judgments
   - Chapters 15 and 16 go together. They are a part of the same vision, describing the seven final plagues, which come out of the seventh trumpet, or the last woe.
   - Chapters 15 and 16 come out of the judgment of the last trumpet. We found part of this in the latter part of chapter 11, about a temple of God that was opened in heaven (11:19). That temple appears again here in these two chapters.
   - The delineation of that judgment is found in chapters 15 and 16.
2. *"And I saw another sign in heaven"* (15:1).
   - In the book of Revelation, there are seven "wonders" or "signs." Here, we find the fifth sign or wonder, at the beginning of the end.
   - In the first verse, two words stand out. The words *"last"* and *"filled,"* or completed.
   - The emphasis in this verse is on the word *"last,"* which, in the original Greek, is spelled *eschatas.* The word *eschatology,* the doctrine of the last things, comes from this word.
   - You will note the word *"filled"* means that the wrath of God completed.
3. The Vision of the Sea Mingled with Fire
   - In verse 2, John *"saw, as it were, a sea of glass mingled with fire."* Such a sea also appeared back in chapter 4, verse 6, but here, it is mingled with fire.
   - Remember, this is a vision and it is also a sign, so when John sees the sea before the throne of God, he sees the people who have come out of great tribulation and trial.
   - The group is clearly identified as those who were victorious over the beast, although it cost them their lives.
   - Here, they stand on the sea of glass, they're singing, and they have the harps of God. They are rejoicing over the fact that they achieved victory over the beast. The kind of triumph that these martyrs of the tribulation will experience is deliverance *through* fire, not *out of* fire.
4. The Song of the Lamb
   - In verse 3, *"they sing the song of Moses the servant of God, and the song of the Lamb."*
   - It is strange that the first recorded song in the Word of God is in chapter 15 of Exodus, the song of Moses. The last recorded song in the Bible is here in chapter 15 of Revelation.
   - In Exodus 15, the children of Israel sing the song of Moses because it is a song of redemption out of bondage.
   - The song of the Lamb in Revelation 15 is a song of redemption from sin.
   - The substance of both songs is of the mighty works of God. Notice some of these words of that song in verse 3:
     a. God is almighty.
     b. He is just and true.
     c. He is the king of saints (this refers to nations, not believers).
     d. He is holy and, for this reason, men should fear and glorify Him.

e. He will be worshipped by the nations, referring to the time of the establishment of the kingdom.

5. The Heavenly Tabernacle

+ In verses 5–8, John's attention is drawn to another breathtaking sight. The heavenly tabernacle, of which the earthly tabernacle and temple were patterned, was thrown open and John was permitted to look into the Holy of Holies.

+ This concept of a tabernacle in heaven has been a difficult thing for many people to understand. Remember that God gave Moses specific instructions on how to build the tabernacle in the wilderness and told him it was to be made from the same pattern as the one in heaven.

+ Sometimes, in Scripture, we are given glimpses of that tabernacle. The writer of Hebrews draws many parallels between the function of the priest in the earthly tabernacle and Christ, our high priest, in the heavenly tabernacle.

+ Look up Revelation 15:5:

_____

_____

_____

_____

+ The temple of the tabernacle of the testimony is referring to the holy place. It is opened so that seven angels are revealed. They are clothed in pure and white linen. They are dressed like priests and, in their hands, they hold the seven golden vials full of the wrath of God.

+ *"Vials"* means a shallow pan, often called *censers*. In them, the wrath of God was placed from off the altar, and incense was poured on top of the coals to burn before God.

+ These golden censers were given to the seven angels by one of the cherubim (one of the four living creatures).

+ You will recall the four living creatures from chapter 6, where they are instruments of judgment. You will remember that one of them said, "Come," and a white horse came on the scene. Then another said, "Come," and the red horse came and so forth. It is these cherubim who give to these seven angels the seven vials or censers of the judgment of God.

+ When the seven angels receive the censers, *"the temple was filled with smoke from the glory of God, and from his power; and no man was able to enter into the temple, till the seven plagues of the seven angels were fulfilled"* (15:8).

+ This means that the great and final interdiction of God has come. All mediation ceases and the great and final unpardonable sin has now been committed—and no man can enter the temple. The door is shut and the temple has become a house of indignation, of wrath, and of judgment until these seven plagues have poured out into the earth.

6. A Closer Look at Tabernacle

+ The tabernacle of the Old Testament was a portable building made of cloth and skins, carried from place to place by the Jews during their forty years in the wilderness and their first few years in the Promised Land.

+ Later, the Jews built their temple in Jerusalem using the same floorplan as that of the tabernacle. The main difference was the materials used in its construction.

+ There was only one gate in the fence that surrounded the tabernacle. Squarely in front of the gate, inside the fence, was the brazen altar of the sacrifice. This showed many that there was only one way to God, and that innocent sacrifice was required for God to bear the guilt and death penalty of the person making the sacrifice.

+ There was only one light inside the building, and that was a candelabrum of God's own design. It was by this light that all of the services of the priest were performed. This single light taught that only God could provide illumination for the understanding of divine truths and worship.

+ There was also an altar of incense, on which the priests were to continually burn incense. The incense was symbolic of the people's prayers.

+ Once a year, the high priest would select a spotless lamb and offer it on the altar for the sins of his people. He would then take some of its blood and go into the tabernacle.

+ He would go into the Holy of Holies and appear before the ark of the covenant, a small, gold, overlaid wooden chest with two golden angelic figures standing upon its lid, facing each other and looking down at the box. Between the two golden angels was a radiant, multicolored light called the presence of God, or the *Shekinah* glory. This was the manifestation of God's presence on earth. No other spot in the world could boast of this special presence of God—only the Jews enjoyed this privilege.

+ On top of the lid of the ark, and beneath the blazing glory of light, was a golden cover called "the mercy seat." It was called this because it was here that the high priest obtained mercy for the people each year as he sprinkled the blood of sacrifice on it.

+ Inside the ark were three objects that God instructed the people keep there:

   a. First were the second tablets of stone on which the Ten Commandments were rewritten by God. Moses angrily broke the original tablets when he came down from Sinai and found the people steeped in sin. These second tablets were put into the ark as a witness to man's rejection of God's perfect moral law.

   b. Second, there was a pot of manna. This was placed there after the people complained about the food that God had provided in the wilderness. They were tired of manna for breakfast, lunch, and dinner, so God had them put a pot of manna in the ark to demonstrate man's rejection of God's provision for daily needs.

   c. Third, there was Aaron's rod that budded. This occurred when a rebel group tried to take over the leadership of the nation from Aaron and Moses. God told the two groups of leaders to stand before the tabernacle and to hold out their rods, the symbol of leadership. God proclaimed that the rod that sprouted, or budded, would be the one He had chosen to be the leader. The rod of Aaron sprouted, so God instructed the people to put this rod in the ark as a witness of man's rejection of God's chosen leadership.

+ When you look on these three things, you find that they are all symbols to the fact that man was sinful and rightfully deserving of God's judgment.

+ All of the people who came by faith in the atonement provided by the Lord God were forgiven and accepted. All of this teaches us that, in the symbolic picture of the tabernacle, we find the figure and type of Jesus Christ, the Lamb of God, whose blood would not merely cover sin but would actually take away the sin of the world, thereby turning the throne of God in heaven's tabernacle into a seat of mercy for all who come by faith in Jesus Christ.

+ You can now understand the shock John must have received when he saw that there had been a sobering change in the character of the sanctuary in heaven. It had now become a place from which the seven final plagues were sent forth. No longer was it a place where men were reconciled to God.

## How Much Do You Remember?

1. What does John's vision of a sea mingled with fire represent?
2. Describe the words found in the Song of the Lamb in Revelation 15:3.
3. Describe what John saw when he beheld the open tabernacle.
4. What was the Jewish tabernacle like? What about their temple that was fashioned after it?
5. Where was the only place that had the Shekinah glory?
6. Which three objects were placed in the ark of the covenant, and why?

## Your Assignment for Next Week:

1. Read Revelation chapter 16.
2. Review your notes from this lesson.
3. Underline your Bible.

## Lesson 17 Notes

_____

_____

_____

_____

_____

_____

_____

_____

_____

_____

_____

_____

_____

_____

_____

_____

_____

_____

_____

_____

_____

# Lesson 18
# REVELATION 16

## The Seven Bowl Judgments

1.  The Commencement
    - In verse 1, we see that God prepares to release the seven final climactic judgments on the earth. They are sent forth by the mighty voice of God booming out of the smoke-filled heavenly temple.
    - Heretofore, these successions of sevens have moved with deliberation. As the seals were broken, there was one, then another, and so forth. When the trumpets were revealed, there was deliberation, one after another.
    - But as the judgments move toward the final climax, they move furiously and quickly. Immediately, these things come to pass.

2.  The First Vial
    - The judgment poured out from the bowl of the first angel is directed upon a specifically singled-out company who had accepted the mark of the beast, that is, the antichrist, and were worshipping his image.
    - The judgment, or plague, is described as intensely painful boils that refused to heal.
    - We know that they didn't heal because we find in verse 11 that the tormented ones are still blaspheming God due to their suffering.

3.  The Second Vial
    - The second vial is in verse 3.
    - You will remember that at the sounding of the second trumpet, one third of the sea became blood and a third part of the sea creatures died.
    - Now, with the outpouring of the second bowl or vial judgment, all of the sea is contaminated so that all the remaining creatures in the sea die.
    - I believe the word "*sea*" means the continuous body of saline water that covers over 70 percent of the exterior of the earth's surface to an average depth of 12,500 feet and, in some places, a maximum depth of 35,800 feet.
    - It staggers the imagination to try to visualize the billions of floating, rotting, dying sea creatures and the awful, unbearable smell.
    - This automatically becomes a congealed mass of blood.

4.  The Third Vial
    - This vial is found in verses 4–7.
    - With the outpouring of the contents of the third bowl, the wrath of God follows the pattern of the third trumpet judgment that fell upon the third part of the rivers and the fountains of waters—that is, earth's freshwater system and the sustainer of human life—because thirst is more terrifying than hunger.
    - All of the springs of sparkling water and the mighty rivers and fountains become blood.
    - God's judgments are final and they are just.
    - In verse 6, you will note that God, the righteous judge, is judging those who shed the blood of saints and prophets. He gives blood to drink for those who killed those saints and prophets.

5. The Fourth Vial
   - This fourth vial is found in verses 8–9.
   - The fourth trumpet judgment had to do with the celestial bodies,—the sun, moon, and stars. Both the light of day and night were darkened by one third.
   - The fourth vial apparently affects the sun alone. The intensity of its heat is increased until it scorches men with its fire.
   - Rather than repent, the men *"blaspheme the name of God, which hath power over these plagues"* (16:9).
   - They know full well that this is the hand of divine judgment, and yet, they repent not.

6. The Fifth Vial
   - The fifth bowl to be poured out by the fifth angel is found in verses 10–11. It is directed at the source of the world's wickedness, namely, the throne of the beast (the antichrist), the seat of satanic power and authority.
   - The result of the judgment is darkness filling his kingdom. Although Satan's kingdom is a kingdom of darkness, this judgment is, undoubtedly, like the thick darkness that covered Egypt in the day of God's plagues, described as *"darkness which may be felt"* (Exodus 10:21).
   - The darkness in this judgment makes the work of the antichrist difficult to the point of the impossible. Adding to the people's misery and their confusion is the continuing pain from the sores of the previous judgment.

7. The Sixth Vial
   - The sixth vial is found in verses 12–16.
   - Here we find judgment upon the great river Euphrates and it is dried up.
   - You will note that the great sections of the book of Revelation end in that final day of the Lord God Almighty, the battle of Armageddon.
   - The visions in chapter 14 end in that great battle of the day of the Lord. Here, in chapters 15 and 16, the visions do the same once again. They end in the great battle of the day of the Lord.
   - In the next section, chapters 17–19, chapter 19 ends in that great battle of the day of the Lord. God's book says that time, history, and government all move toward a final conflict in this earth.
   - The strange thing about this particular battle, as revealed in Scripture, is that all the armies and leaders are gathered in Palestine.
   - The sixth trumpet says one of those armies numbers two hundred million men. (See Revelation 9:16.)
   - You'll note in Revelation 16:12 that God explains His purpose in drying up the river: *"that the way of the kings of the east might be prepared."*
   - In the rest of this vial, we learn that all the kings of the world are preparing to be at the same place. No strategy on the part of any government or rulers would ever bring such a thing about. So how do they get there? The book of Revelation explains the situation.
   - Revelation 16:13–14 says, *"I saw three unclean spirits like frogs come out of the mouth of the dragon, and out of the mouth of the beast, and out of the mouth of the false prophet…. which go forth unto the kings of the earth and of the whole world, to gather them to the battle of that great day of God Almighty."*
   - The trinity of evil spirits is going to persuade those armies and those leaders to gather in Israel, where the final battle shall be fought. Evil deception brought them to the battle. In verse 16, God brings them to Armageddon.

8. The Seventh Vial
   - The seventh vial is found in verses 17–21.

- The contents of the seventh and last judgment were not directed to one certain location, but to the entire atmosphere surrounding the whole earth, thus, the result of the outpouring was a worldwide catastrophe.

- Voices, thunder, lightning, and a violent earthquake shall be a part of this last judgment. The cities and towns shall be swallowed up, with special emphasis on the city of Babylon, *"to give unto her the cup of the wine of the fierceness of his wrath"* (16:19), which we shall see in the next two chapters.

- The voice from the throne in heaven declares, *"It is done"* (16:17). With all of the pain and terror, and the awful judgments of God, men still blaspheme God because of the plague of the hail storm. The last and final judgment concludes with blind, hard-hearted men blaspheming the name of our Lord and Savior.

## How Much Do You Remember?

1. These vial judgments succeed differently than the seals and trumpets. How do they progress?
2. Who is the first vial judgment directed toward and what does this plague consist of?
3. What happens to the sea with the second vial?
4. Who is being judged in the third vial and what plague will they face?
5. What will happen to the sun in the fourth vial?
6. Describe the pouring out of the fifth bowl.
7. How do all of the kings of the world gather in the same place for the sixth vial?
8. What disasters will occur to the whole earth in the last vial judgment?

## Your Assignment for Next Week:

1. Read Revelation chapter 17.
2. Review your notes from this lesson.
3. Underline your Bible.

## Lesson 18 Notes

_____

_____

_____

_____

_____

_____

_____

_____

_____

_____

_____

_____

_____

_____

_____

_____

_____

_____

# Lesson 19
# REVELATION 17

## Ecclesiastical Babylon

1.  An Introduction to Babylon

    *   Babylon is one of the most discussed subjects in the entire Word of God. Babylon is referred to more than 260 times in Scripture.

    *   As we get into the study of Babylon, chapters 17 and 18 go together, yet there is a vast difference between the content of these chapters.

    *   In this description of the destruction of Babylon, neither kings nor the governments of the earth are mentioned. This is the intervention of God.

    *   The destruction of Babylon was referred to in Revelation 14:8 and 16:9, but it is described in detail here in chapters 17 and 18.

    *   The emphasis in chapter 17 is on religious Babylon. Babylon is both a city and a system. Chapter 17 is about the system and chapter 18 is about the city.

    *   Babylon had its beginnings with the building of the Tower of Babel in Genesis 10:10. It later flourished under Nebuchadnezzar.

    *   There are three theories for what Babylon represents, and I have come to the conclusion that all three of the following interpretations could be true, as far a man is concerned. But could it be true as far as Scripture is concerned?

        a.  Some scholars believe that this Babylon is to be physically rebuilt on the banks of the Euphrates River at the head of the Persian Gulf.

        b.  Second, there are those who believe that this Babylon represents a system of life and culture whose essential principal is alienation from God. They believe that it could represent a great city anywhere in the world.

        c.  Third are those who believe Babylon represents the social, cultural, and commercial life of the end times and that this entire system is summarized in one great world city called Babylon.

    *   The name *Babylon* is used for more than a city in these chapters; it also stands for a system. This is much like Americans speak of Wall Street and Madison Avenue. Although they are actual streets, they also stand for the financial and advertising enterprises of our nation.

2.  Many Waters

    *   Verse 1 begins with one of the seven bowl angels who had part in the seven vials.

    *   This angel speaks to John, saying, *"Come hither; I will shew unto thee the judgment of the great whore that sitteth upon many waters."* The *"many waters"* is indicative of many nations—the entire population of the world. Verse 15 also reiterates this definition of many waters. Look up this verse:

    _____

    _____

    _____

    _____

3. Historical Babylon

- In verse 2, Babylon, this *"great whore"* (17:1), symbolizes the false religious system that is so appealing, she has been able to seduce all the kings of the earth with her deception.

- How is this religious system, called *Babylon*, able to attract the leaders, both religious and political, to follow her? What was it about Babylon of old that this great false religion will emulate? The answer is unveiled in the first meaning of the word *Babylon*.

- The first Babylon began on the plains of Shinar, where the first world dictator established the world's first religious center. The dictator's name was *Nimrod*, which means "we will revolt." He is described as *"a mighty hunter before the LORD"* (Genesis 10:9).

- The beginning of his kingdom was Babylon. (See Genesis 10–11.)

- Under Nimrod, the first united religious act was performed—the building of *"a tower, whose top may reach unto heaven"* (Genesis 11:4).

- The tower of Babel, as built by Nimrod, was an astrological observatory. Centuries later, God pronounced judgment on Babylon, when He said, in essence, "She had labored with sorceries, and astrology from her youth"—indicating that these were practiced in Babylon from the beginning of history. (See Isaiah 47:12–13.)

- Now, in the book of Revelation, we are told what John saw, so we can better understand what religious Babylon is all about.

4. The Woman on the Beast

- In verse 3, John sees a woman sitting on a beast. The beast is clearly meant to be the man of sin, the antichrist of Revelation 13:1–10. We know this because we can compare the beast of verse 3 with the beast described in verse 1 of chapter 13.

- The startling feature of this scene is that the whore is sitting on the beast, indicating that she will have power over the man of sin.

- This event must occur before the man of sin overthrows all existing religions and requires everyone to worship him.

- You will notice, at the beginning of verse 3, that John is *"carried…away in spirit into the wilderness."* Wherever there is spiritual adultery, there is desolation and a desert of dreary waste.

- In verse 4, we see that this harlot is bedecked with splendor, signifying glory and wealth, and she holds in her hand a cup of abomination, filthiness, and fornication.

5. A Mystery

- In verse 5, her name is called *"MYSTERY."* This is not an adjective but part of her name: *"MYSTERY, BABYLON."*

- Because of the word *"MYSTERY,"* this Babylon is not referring to a city on the Euphrates. The use of this word will be explained further in verses 9 and 18. Since the true church is also called a *"mystery"* (Ephesians 5:32), this apostate church is a counterfeit of that.

- The harlot is also the mother of harlots. In other words, many groups will come together under one adulterous, federated church.

- The identification of *"seven mountains"* in verse 9 creates an interrelation of Babylon and Rome, the "city on seven hills." One could immediately draw the conclusion that the Roman Church is the harlot.

- But this is not necessarily the whole picture, for the apostate church is not merely the Roman Church. It will include other groups. The tie that will bind them together will be their adulterous method of running every kingdom of the world.

6. The Blood of the Saints and Martyrs
   - In verse 6, the terrible words are recorded: *"And I saw the woman drunken with the blood of the saints, and with the blood of the martyrs of Jesus."*
   - In this vision, John sees the blood of the saints and martyrs, which is shed by that rich, scarlet, and idolatrous church, and John *"wondered with a great admiration."*
7. An Explanation
   - In verse 7, the angel says to John, *"Wherefore didst thou marvel?"* And then he says, *"I will tell thee the mystery of the woman, and of the beast."*
   - The angel promises John an explanation of the vision he had seen. This explanation begins in the next verse.
   - Verse 8 identifies the beast. He is the same one referred to in Revelation 11:7 as one coming out of the abyss. Here, he is said to *"ascend out of the bottomless pit,"* indicating that these chapters are not chronological, but written only as John sees them. This indicates that verses 1–7 precede the beast's rise to power in the middle of the tribulation period.
   - In verses 9–11, the seven heads of the beast are identified as the seven mountains on which the harlot sits. No doubt can be entertained as to the meaning of these words. The seven hills of Rome were a common identification for Rome by writers in history. In other words, the center of the beast's power is Rome.
   - In verse 10, John continues with his interpretation of verses 1–7, when he says, *"There are seven kings: five are fallen, and one is, and the other is not yet come; and when he cometh, he must continue a short space."* Thus, the seven heads represent seven kingdoms: five existing prior to John's day, one existing in his day, and another one yet to come. This is referring to those great world empires since the time of the original Babylon.
   - Once again, interpreting this, we see the following:
     a. The first kingdom was Assyria, with its occult capital city of Nineveh.
     b. The second was Egypt, with its pyramids built according to astrological specifications.
     c. Third was the Babylonian Empire, with its perfection of the black arts.
     d. Fourth was Medo-Persia, which was eventually enslaved by the Babylonian religion.
     e. Fifth was the Greek Empire, with her idolatrous religions and ancient temple.
   - *"One is"* refers to Rome. Rome was filled with the same occultic beliefs as Babylon. This was the sixth kingdom of John's vision.
   - John looks to the future when he says of the seventh head or the seventh kingdom that *"the other is not yet come; and when he cometh, he must continue a short space"* (verse 10).
   - This seventh kingdom refers to the future revival of the Roman Empire. The seventh head is different from the other six because it has ten horns on it. This indicates that the seventh kingdom will be made up of ten nations from the old Roman Empire, which will have confederated into one political unit. This revived Roman Empire of ten nations will be dominated by the same Babylonish religious system that has been in existence since Nimrod's day.
   - In verse 11, we find another kingdom, which is referred to as *"the eighth, and is of the seven,"* which means that, briefly, there will sprout another kingdom that will be an outgrowth of the seventh.
   - This speaks of the brief reign of the antichrist himself. He will emerge in full bloom during the last half of the tribulation. That is the reason he is referred to as receiving power of the kings for one hour. When the antichrist becomes indwelt with Satan at the middle of the tribulation, his kingdom

will take a different tone from that point on. The whole world will worship this particular beast, the eighth kingdom, instead of the harlot—the apostate church.

- At the middle of the tribulation, this outgrowth of the seventh kingdom, the antichrist working with the false prophet, finds that he no longer needs support of the religious system. Possessed by Satan, he proclaims himself to be God, seated in the temple in Jerusalem. He will turn on the great harlot, ecclesiastical Babylon, and destroy her.

8. An Explanation of the Ten Kings
    - In verses 12–14, we find clear explanation of the ten kings.
    - Look up Revelation 17:12:

    _____

    _____

    _____

    _____

    - *"One hour"* should be understood as meaning one purpose or one brief activity. These kings appear to act as independent entities but, according to verse 13, they have one mind and give all their power and authority to the antichrist.
    - Their one purpose of giving the strength to the beast is defined in verse 14: *"These shall make war with the Lamb."*
    - The Lamb shall overcome them, for, according to verse 14, *"he is Lord of lords, and King of kings: and they that are with him are called, and chosen, and faithful."*
    - In other words, John sees the Lamb as overcoming the antichrist in this vision.

9. An Explanation of the Waters
    - The waters on which the harlot sits are now explained in verse 15, as we saw in verse 1.
    - They are defined as being the peoples of the world.
    - The apostate church shall be ecumenical, made up of all denominations and faiths.

10. The Destruction of Ecclesiastical Babel
    - In verses 16–18, we see the destruction of Babel.
    - Religious Babylon who sought political alliances and powers, will, in the end, be destroyed by a great political alliance.
    - These ten nations *"shall hate the great whore, and shall make her desolate."* The words *"desolate"*, *"naked"*, and *"burn"* all reveal the extent of her annihilation.
    - In verse 17, it is God who will incline them to align themselves with the beast *"until the words of God shall be fulfilled."*
    - Religion shall flourish during the first part of the tribulation in the false system called Babylon, the harlot.
    - The system shall center itself in Rome, and shall include other harlot groups. It will exercise great political influence.
    - We have seen that the man of sin, with his ten league nations, will destroy the harlot, ecclesiastical Babylon, and set himself up to be worshipped.

## How Much Do You Remember?

1. What does chapter 17 emphasize about Babylon that chapter 18 will not?
2. What are the three ideas about what Babylon represents?
3. In verse 2, what does Babylon symbolize?
4. What do the seven heads of the beast represent, and where is the center of the beast's power?
5. The seventh kingdom represents the future revival of which empire?
6. How will religious Babylon be destroyed?

## Your Assignment for Next Week:

1. Read Revelation chapter 18.
2. Review your notes from this lesson.
3. Underline your Bible.

## Lesson 19 Notes

_____

_____

_____

_____

_____

_____

_____

_____

_____

_____

_____

_____

_____

_____

_____

_____

_____

_____

_____

_____

_____

# Lesson 20
# REVELATION 18

## God's Judgment upon Babylon—The Commercial and Political Babylon

In chapter 17, ecclesiastical Babylon was destroyed by the political alliance of the ten nations who shall hate the great whore and make her desolate. The kings voluntarily join forces to destroy the harlot, but in doing so, they fulfill the purpose of God. (See Revelation 17:17.)

Babylon involves a city—that is certain—and it also involves a system. The religious aspect of that system was described in chapter 17. This chapter concerns the other Babylon, which will be the center of the social, political, cultural, and commercial life of the entire globe.

In this lesson, we will explain the verses and then go back and consider the four great judgments of God upon Babylon. Remember that the judgment of this Babylon is by the hand of God, not the hand of man.

1. *"Babylon the great is fallen"* (18:2).

   • In verse 1, we see another angel come down from heaven with great power. This announcement is made *"after these things"*—the things of chapter 17.

   • In verse 2, the angel cries with a mighty voice, saying, *"Babylon the great is fallen, is fallen."* The angel announces that Babylon is demonic. This is emphasized in three ways:

     a. First, it is *"the habitation of devils."*

     b. Second, it is *"the hold [prison] of every fowl spirit."*

     c. Third, it is *"a cage [prison] of every unclean and hateful bird."* This phrase alludes to the bird in the parable of the mustard seed—indicating the demonic forces at work in the apostate system.

2. *"For all nations have drunk of the wine of the wrath of her fornication, and the kings of the earth have committed fornication with her, and the merchants of the earth are waxed rich through the abundance of her delicacies"* (18:3).

   • In verse 3, we find the charge of fornication or unfaithfulness to the Lord, which is repeated from chapter 17.

   • Babylon is intoxicating. All nations drink of the wine of her unfaithfulness. Merchants particularly fall prey to her.

   • Even kings commit fornication with her (spiritual adultery).

   • Big business becomes even wealthier because of the *"abundance of her delicacies."*

3. *"Come out of her, my people, that ye be not partakers of her sins, and that ye receive not of her plagues"* (18:4).

   • In verse 4, there is a call from a voice in heaven asking Babylon to come out and not to partake of her sin, to escape judgment.

   • This is a call to those living in the days of tribulation who have not received the mark of the beast.

   • Its application is always relevant to believers in every age not to compromise with Satan's world system in any way.

4. Verses 5–8

   • In verses 5–8, we find an appeal for separation on the basis of three things:

     a. First, the sins of Babylon have *"reached unto heaven, and God hath remembered."*

    b.   Second, in verse 6, God shall render unto her what she, Babylon, has given out. Judgment will be doubled because of her works. Even the cup of sin and spiritual adultery she has filled will be doubled.

    c.   Third, in verses 7–8, in the place of glory and luxury with which she has clothed herself, God will retaliate with torment and sorrow. The word *"deliciously"* means *"luxuriously."* In place of Babylon's assumed position, as a queen with many lovers, God gives plagues, death, mourning, and famine.

- In verse 8, you will notice that *"her plagues come in one day."* Besides death, mourning, and famine, *"she shall be utterly burned with fire."*

- Strong is the Lord God, who judges sin and judges Babylon.

5.   Verses 9–10

- In verses 9–10, we find the first lament from the kings of the earth.

- They weep and wail when they see the smoke of the fire.

- Note that these so-called kings of the earth, who had committed fornication with the ecclesiastical Babylon, are now *"standing afar off."* They are trying to avoid doom, but, in reality, they only postpone it.

- The swiftness of the judgment is emphasized in the phrase *"in one hour."* The judgment shall be rapid—like a nuclear weapon.

6.   Verses 11–17

- Here, we get another view of the destruction of Babylon.

- In verse 11, the merchants of the earth weep and sorrow because of the fall of this commercial Babylon. Now no one will buy, and the merchants will lose all they have.

- In verses 12–13, we find a list of twenty-eight items that will no longer be purchased. Those twenty-eight articles begin with gold and silver and end with the *"souls of men."*

- One feature you should note about these items is that they are all luxury items. Also, the final item means that merchants will be trafficking in people as well as things.

- In verse 14, everything they had thought to be important, and everything that their soul lusted for, had departed from them. *"All things which were dainty and goodly are departed"* from them, and they will never have them again.

- In verse 15, all the merchants who were made rich by this great city—the commercial Babylon—will do the same things as the kings did in an earlier verse. They *"stand afar off for the fear of her torment, weeping and wailing."*

- In verses 16–17, these same merchants cry, *"Alas, alas that great city, that was clothed in fine linen, and purple, and scarlet, and decked with gold, and precious stones, and pearls! For in one hour so great riches is come to nought."*

- All of the stock markets crash on a worldwide scale and, as usual, unsaved men turn to their own interests and devise how they might recover some of what they lost.

7.   Verses 17–19

- In the last part of verse 17, we see that all those connected with commerce on the seas also cry and lament over the destruction of Babylon.

- This includes shipmasters (owners), sailors, and all who work on ships. Their weeping is for the same reason—their careers are suddenly destroyed.

- In verse 18, notice that they looked upon the city that was burning. They saw the smoke and cry out, *"What city is like unto this great city!"*

- Then, in verse 19, they cast dust on their heads, weep some more, and cry out again, *"Alas that great city, wherein were made rich all that had ships in the sea by reason of her costliness! for in one hour is she made desolate."*
- Notice that terminology, over and over again in this chapter—*"one hour."* This shows the rapid and immediate judgment of God Almighty on the city of Babylon.

8.  Verses 20–24
- The reaction of the world to the destruction of Babylon, with all of its business interests, is clearly set forth.
- The world weeps, for the materials things are all that they have. All these things are destroyed; all is lost.
- The reaction of heaven to the destruction of Babylon is also recorded.
- Whereas the kings, merchants, and all of the people in the city of Babylon mourned and grieved because of the passing of Babylon, heaven and the friends of heaven rejoice.
- In verse 20, it should read, "Ye saints and apostles and prophets." Also, in verse 20, it says, *"God hath avenged you on her."* That is, God has judged your case against Babylon. Babylon has slain the saints; now God slays Babylon.
- Here is the final answer to the plea of the martyrs back in Revelation 6:9–11. Then, as if to reassure the citizens of heaven that the destruction is final, an angel takes a millstone and casts it into the sea, to symbolize the sure and complete destruction of Babylon in verse 21.
- This act brings forth a funeral dirge concerning the judgment upon Babylon. You will notice this in verses 22–23. There will be no music, no worker, no machinery, no light, and no happiness found in Babylon anymore. The reason is twofold: Babylon deceived the nations and killed the saints.

9.  Four Reasons for the Destruction of Babylon
- Why is it that God's judgment so terribly falls upon this city? There are four reasons:
    a.  The first reason is described in verse 5: *"For her sins have reached unto heaven, and God hath remembered her iniquities."*
        - In the first Babel, their infamous tower was built block by block and brick by brick, up and up and up, until Nimrod proposed to reach heaven with it.
        - That evil, God says, has come before His remembrance. The words, *"have reached unto heaven"* are remembered by the Lord God.
        - Like the sin of wicked Babylon, building up and up and up has made her mighty because of her materialism, secularism, godlessness, and denial of Christ.
        - Babylon's sins have reached unto heaven like the tower of Babel, and God has remembered her iniquities. That's the first reason.
    b.  The second reason for the judgment of God is described in verse 7: *"How much she hath glorified herself and lived deliciously, so much torment and sorrow give her: for she saith in her heart, I sit a queen, and am no widow, and shall see no sorrow."*
        - In that arrogance, self-conceit, and self-glorification, she boasts of her atheism and her infidelity to the Lord God.
        - To her, there is no such a thing as God; there is not a Christ and there is not a Holy Spirit.
        - She proposes for herself dominance in history and, in the future, her reign will last forever.
        - The false, self-glorification in a boasting that defies God is another reason for Babylon's judgment.

c. A third reason for the destruction of this great city is described in verses 12–13. In them are listed twenty-eight articles of merchandise.

- The enumeration starts with gold and closes with *"souls of men."* Souls, used as merchandise that one would pack up and ship out.

- To Babylon, the lives and the souls of men are merely matters of commerce.

- As we increase in our culture, and as we go further and further into achievements and civilizations, God says that our culture shall become more merciless, more ruthless and God-dishonoring.

- With the interest even now on the things mentioned in verses 11–12, such as gold and precious stones, fine linen and silk, all manners of fine wood, ivory, brass and marble, odors and ointments, wine, oil, and flour, sheep, horses, chariots, and even the bodies of individuals— can you imagine what it shall be like then as compared to now?

d. The fourth reason for God's judgment on Babylon is stated in verse 24, which we have briefly covered. Babylon will have killed the prophets, saints, and all the men that were slain upon the earth.

- The system and the demonic power of Babylon would have done away with the blood of all of those who would not receive the mark of the beast.

- An example comes from Matthew 23, where our Lord is condemning the scribes and Pharisees. He says that upon the city of Jerusalem will come all the blood shed since the blood of Abel to the blood of Zechariah, *"whom ye slew between the temple and the altar"* (Matthew 23:35).

- Upon that generation, and upon that city, will come all the blood of the prophets and of all of the saints that was shed from the days of Abel to the days of Zechariah.

10. A Review of Chapters 17 and 18

- To finalize what we have studied looking back through chapters 17 and 18, we find, and I believe, that the capital city of the Roman Empire shall be the economic, commercial giant as described in this chapter 18.

- The harlot of chapter 17 is not a city; it is an occultic religious system and an influence that exists in a spiritually adulterous relationship between the city and the kingdom of the antichrist during the first half of the tribulation.

- At the end of the tribulation, the capital of the revived Roman Empire, the subject of chapter 18, shall be destroyed by God Himself. How He disposes of the antichrist and the false prophet shall be a part of our study in the next chapter.

## How Much Do You Remember?

1. The phrase *"in one hour"* is repeated in this chapter. What significance does it have?
2. The list of twenty-eight articles that will no longer be purchased begins with gold and ends with what?
3. Look back to verses 20–24. Why will the world weep?
4. What are the four reasons for the destruction of Babylon?

## Your Assignment for Next Week:

1. Read Revelation chapter 19.
2. Review your notes from this lesson.
3. Underline your Bible.

## Lesson 20 Notes

_____

_____

_____

_____

_____

_____

_____

_____

_____

_____

_____

_____

_____

_____

_____

_____

_____

_____

_____

# Lesson 21
# REVELATION 19

The Marriage of the Lamb, the Second Coming of Christ, and the Battle of Armageddon

1. Joy in Heaven (verses 1-6)
   - There are four *Alleluias* in this brief portion of Scripture, which indicates that there will be joy in heaven after the occurrences in chapters 17 and 18.
   a. The first alleluia is over the destruction of the great whore, Mystery Babylon, the scarlet woman with the golden cup in her hand. When she is destroyed, all heaven says, *"Alleluia."* (See verses 1–2.)
   b. The second alleluia is over the destruction of the city, Babylon. The iniquity of Babylon lies heavy on the heart of God's universe and when she is annihilated, all heaven feels the triumph of the glory and grace of God. *"And again they said, Alleluia. And her smoke rose up for ever and ever"* (19:3).
   c. The next alleluia is found in verse 4. It is uttered by the exalted and glorified creation of our Lord in heaven: *"And the four and twenty elders and the four beasts fell down and worshipped God that sat on the throne, saying, Amen; Alleluia."*
      - Notice that word: *"Amen."* It is the special word of sacred ratification, of holy acquiescence. It continues as the sealing word of the Gospels and the epistles. It is the heavenly word of avowal, of committal to truth. It seals, it affirms, and it binds. It is the highest word of praise that human speech can utter.
      - Human utterance could go no higher than "amen." It is thus with the twenty-four elders and the four cherubim, who are most intimately connected with the throne of God.
   d. The fourth alleluia is found in verses 5–6. It is uttered in an answer to a call from the throne itself, and that call is found in verse 5, where we read, *"And a voice came out of the throne, saying, Praise our God, all ye his servants, and ye that fear him, both small and great."*
      - The mighty answering voice of the vast, innumerable multitude surrounding the throne sounded like the roar and the thunder of many waters. The throng cried in thunderous exaltation, *"Alleluia: for the Lord God omnipotent reigneth."*

2. The Marriage of the Lamb (verses 7–10)
   - After the four alleluias of great joy in heaven, there comes one of the sweet portions of Scripture, which begins in verse 7.
   - Notice that there is gladness and rejoicing because the marriage of the Lamb is come and His wife—the church—has made herself ready. That church shall be arrayed in fine linen, clean and white, for her fine linen is the righteousness of the saints.
   a. The Bridegroom
      - At the marriage of the Lamb, we are first introduced to the Bridegroom. The Bridegroom is Christ, referred to as *"the Lamb,"* a description of His blood-bought redemptive relationship with us, who have been saved by His grace.
   b. The bride
      - The bride is the church of our Lord Jesus Christ.

- The bride is not the Old Testament Israel. Old Testament Israel is described in Isaiah and Hosea as the adulterous wife of Jehovah, but she shall be the forgiven and restored wife—and a forgiven and a restored wife could neither be called a virgin or a bride.

- The bride married to our Lord is the church, the household of Christian faith. Out of all the languages, tribes, peoples, and families of the earth, among the Jews, from the Gentiles, among the barbarians and the provincials over the earth, God is now calling out a people for His name, that He might present them unto the Lord at the marriage day of the Lamb. The bride is His church.

- God is now preparing his church for that celestial presentation found here in verse 8: *"And to her was granted that she should be arrayed in fine linen, clean and white: for the fine linen is the righteousness of saints."*

- The text also says, in verse 7, *"his wife hath made herself ready."* She has her garments, beautiful and white, prepared for her marriage with her Lord. She made herself ready when she accepted Christ as a personal Savior and became a part of the body of the Lord Jesus.

- Then, after that acceptance of Christ, she made herself ready by functioning as a part of that body by spreading the gospel, teaching the Word, and winning the lost. This is referred to as the judgment seat of Christ, or the rewards of the Christian.

c. The marriage

- Concerning the marriage itself, is it not strange that God does not include it? Nothing is said about it; no word is used to describe it.

- Verse 7 says, *"the marriage of the Lamb is come,"* and that is all. Just the fact of it.

- John hears the alleluia chorus announcing it. He has a word to say about the wife, the bride of Christ, who has made herself ready, but he never recounts the actual wedding itself. The event just happens and all heaven bursts into alleluias concerning it.

3. Speculating About the Marriage

- In Revelation 21:9–10, we read,

*And there came unto me one of the seven angels which had the seven vials full of the seven last plagues, and talked with me, saying, Come hither, I will shew thee the bride, the Lamb's wife. And he carried me away in the spirit to a great and high mountain, and shewed me that great city, the holy Jerusalem, descending out of heaven from God.*

Revelation 21:2 adds that holy Jerusalem was *"prepared as a bride adorned for her husband."*

- That's all we read about it. But there are other facets and aspects of the marriage we ought to consider:

a. The guests

- We ought to consider the guests and the marriage supper in verse 9: *"And he saith unto me,* [this is after the marriage] *Write, Blessed are they which are called unto the marriage supper of the Lamb."*

- The wedding and marriage are one thing, but the supper, the feast and the refreshments, is something altogether different. The bride is wed, the guests dine, and the angels are spectators—there are three different groups.

- You will note at the beginning of verse 9: *"And he* [the angel who is revealing all of this to John] *saith unto me."* That angel said, *"Write, Blessed are they which are called unto the marriage supper of the Lamb. And he saith unto me, These are the true sayings of God."*

- Had all the saved of all time been the bride, then the angel would have told John to write something like this: "Blessed are they who are the wife, who are the bride, of the Lamb." But he did not do any such thing. After he announces the wedding of the Lamb, and after it is over, he then says, *"Blessed are they which are called unto the marriage supper of the Lamb."* The supper is something altogether different from the marriage.

- The blessedness in this beatitude of Revelation 19:9 covers a greater, broader group than is represented by the bride.

- For example, John the Baptist. John the Baptist died before the cross. He was never a part of the visible church of Jesus Christ. He belonged to the old dispensation. That is why the great John the Baptist says, in John 3:29, *"He that hath the bride is the bridegroom: but the friend of the bridegroom, which standeth and heareth him, rejoiceth greatly because of the bridegroom's voice: this my joy therefore is fulfilled."*

- John the Baptist is not a part of the bride. He is not a part of the church. John is a guest. John is a friend who stands and rejoices in the favor of God upon the married couple.

- This is why, I think, in Matthew 11:11, speaking of John the Baptist, our Lord says, *"Verily I say unto you, Among them that are born of women there hath not risen a greater than John the Baptist: [but] he that is least in the kingdom of heaven* [in the dispensation and age of our Lord's church] *is greater than he."* Why is this? Because the least of us who has been saved, the humblest, belongs to the bride of our Lord. We belong to His church. These others are guests invited to witness and celebrate the marriage supper of the Lamb, but they do not belong to this age of grace.

- But, lest someone think that they are less honored and less blessed, these guests of the old dispensation, John was commanded to write a special blessing for them: *"Blessed are they* [the guests] *which are called unto the marriage supper of the Lamb."* This is a special blessing for the saved of the old covenant.

- With holy imagination, we can see the guests come into the marriage supper of the Lamb. I suppose John the Baptist will be honored among all. He comes in along with Abraham and Isaiah and all the Old Testament prophets, as well as all of God's children who lived under the old covenant. They sit down and break bread with the bride in that glorious day of our blessed Lord.

b. The banquet

- The banquet is called the marriage supper of the Lamb.

- In Luke 22:15–16, as the Lord sat down with His disciples at the Passover, Jesus said, *"With desire I have desired to eat this passover with you before I suffer: for I say unto you, I will not any more eat thereof, until it be fulfilled in the kingdom of God."*

- Jesus also said this at the feast when He instituted the Lord's Supper: *"I say unto you, I will not drink henceforth of this fruit of the vine, until that day when I drink it new with you in my Father's kingdom"* (Matthew 26:29).

- These passages look forward to the marriage of the Lamb—*"when I drink it new with you,"* a new kind of drink.

- Remember John 2:9, when Jesus turned water into wine: *"When the ruler of the feast had tasted the water that was made wine, and knew not whence it was.'"* How was it different? It is the kind that we shall drink at the marriage supper of the Lamb. A delicious, heavenly wine prepared by the hand of God.

- Thus it will be when we gather around the table of the Lord to break bread and drink the fruit of the vine. This story is a prophecy and a foretaste of that beautiful, heavenly banquet when we sit down with our Lord at the marriage supper of the Lamb.

4. The Coming of the Lord and the Battle of Armageddon
   - These two stories go together because the Lord comes in the midst of that terrible and indescribable conflict called the battle of Armageddon.

   a. The coming of the Lord
      - He is the Son of God who bursts the heavens open and appears is thus described: "His eyes were as a flame of fire, and on his head were many crowns" (verse 12).
      - Next, we read, "…and he had a name written, that no man knew, but he himself" (verse 12). This refers to His essential deity, the unknowable and unpronounceable name of God. But we do know that He is the very Lord God who is coming, for Christ Jesus is God of this universe. We are not going to see three Gods in heaven. There is one great Lord God. We know Him as our Father, as our Savior, and as the Holy Spirit in our hearts.
      - In verse 13: "And he was clothed with a vesture dipped in blood [the blood of His enemies]: and his name is called, The Word of God." This is His pronounceable name—the name by which we who are mortal know Him. He became incarnate and we saw His glory as the glory of the only begotten of the Father, full of grace and truth. This is "The Word of God," the Lord Jesus Christ.
      - In verse 15: "And out of his mouth goeth a sharp sword, that with it he should smite the nations." He speaks and things happen.
      - He has strength and power because, also in verse 15, we read, "he shall rule them with a rod of iron: and he treadeth the winepress of the fierceness and wrath of Almighty God." This is the day of judgment. Then John sees His name written as King of Kings and Lord of Lord.
      - John describes the saints that come with Him in verse 14: "And the armies which were in heaven followed him upon white horses, clothed in fine linen, white and clean." We have already been introduced to those saints in Revelation 19:8. They are all the believers who live and are saved in our dispensation, the church age.

   b. The battle of Armageddon
      - The battle of Armageddon begins at verse 17 and ends abruptly.
      - The battle of Armageddon is the scene in which the great God and Savior, Our Lord Jesus Christ, appears to intervene in human history.
      - The first verses of the chapter recount the marriage supper of the Lamb, which is preceded by the marriage of the Son of God to His bride.
      - Immediately after the marriage and the supper, the gates of heaven burst open in the triumph of the hosts of glory.
      - Immediately after the wedding supper, our Lord appears in glory with His angelic host and with His saints. He intervenes in this awesome, catastrophic holocaust.
      - Notice that history does not quietly and gradually merge into the kingdom of our Lord. The end comes violently; it comes in fury.
      - We have seen this battle described before in the book of Revelation. You can find these references in Revelation 9:16, 11:15, 14:17–29, and 16:12–16; and here in Revelation 19.
      - This battle, the final conflict that dissolves human history, is referred to, time and again, in the Old Testament.

- All the prophets, with one accord, say that the armies of the earth will be assembled in Palestine. The king of the north is coming down—perhaps Russia. The king of the west is coming over—perhaps the confederated European states. The kings of the east shall come—perhaps China. The king of the south is coming—perhaps the African nations. All of these will assemble at Megiddo, which is the battlefield of the world.

- We know how they are gathered because we have found the answer in Revelation 16:13, 14, and 16.

- John describes the armies that are warring against the Lord Christ. He does not see the battle, only the angel who stands in the sun, stationed in glory, calling for the fouls and the birds of the heavens to come. (See verse 17.)

- The actual war itself is only described to John as he watches the angel who makes that awful announcement. The vultures of the earth come when the earth is bathed in blood.

- Then John describes what the angel described—the armies that are warring against the Lord in verse 19: *"And I saw the beast, and the kings of the earth, and their armies, gathered together to make war against him that sat on the horse, and against his army."*

- This trio, the beast, the kings, and the false prophet, is leading the opposition to the Lord God. But they don't last long because the invincible warrior, Christ, always is triumphant. The war is over quickly, as we read in verse 20.

- Look at how the battle is fought in verse 20 and copy down this verse:

_____

_____

_____

_____

_____

- The beast is taken. God takes him. And with him, the false prophet is also taken. Both are cast alive into the lake of fire, burning with brimstone. Then, finally, the remnant—the remaining kings—are slain, as the birds fill themselves with the flesh. (See verse 21.)

## How Much Do You Remember?

1. What are the four hallelujahs found in verses 1–6?
2. Who are the Bridegroom and bride in the marriage of the Lamb?
3. How does the bride make herself ready?
4. When speculating about the marriage supper, who will be guests that are called to attend?
5. What happens speedily and immediately after the marriage supper?
6. What information is provided to us about the battle of Armageddon? How and where will it take place?

## Your Assignment for Next Week:

1. Read Revelation chapter 20.
2. Review your notes from this lesson.
3. Underline your Bible.

## Lesson 21 Notes

_____

_____

_____

_____

_____

_____

_____

_____

_____

_____

_____

_____

_____

_____

_____

_____

_____

_____

# Lesson 22
# REVELATION 20

The Binding and Loosing of Satan—The First and Second Resurrections—The Glorious Millennium—The White Throne Judgment—The Second Death

In chapter 20, we find five lessons in only fifteen verses of Scripture. They cover some of the most important subjects we are faced with as Christians. The chapter is split into the subjects listed above, but they are not in continual form.

1.  A Brief Review of the Battle of Armageddon
    *   Chapter 19 of Revelation closed with the battle of Armageddon, in which the Lord God intervened openly and publicly in human history through the coming of Christ.
    *   In that war, in which the antichrist and the false prophet led the kings and the armies of the earth, there is indescribable bloodshed. The enemies of God are destroyed, and the antichrist and false prophet are cast into the lake of hellfire and brimstone.
    *   Beyond the antichrist and false prophet, and beyond the kings, armies, and nations of the earth, there is a sinister, cunning personality who has led them into the winepress of the wrath and the judgment of the almighty God. It is due to this cunning deception that these have been brought to that ultimate and final rejection of God and their open warfare against heaven.

2.  The Binding of Satan (verses 1–3)
    *   What about this cunning, unusual, gifted, and subtle deceiver? Does he escape? The answer is found in Revelation 20. God has singled him out and marked him for a special judgment and damnation. This is the binding of Satan, the enemy of the people of the Lord.
    *   In verses 1–3, you find some unusual words and phrases:

        *And I [John] saw an angel come down from heaven, having the key of the bottomless pit and a great chain in his hand. And he laid hold on the dragon, that old serpent, which is the Devil, and Satan, and bound him a thousand years. And cast him into the bottomless pit, and shut him up, and set a seal upon him.*

    *   The angel of the Lord came down with the key to the "abyss," which is the actual Greek word used. The angel came to lock up Satan in the bottomless pit.
    *   The angel had in his hand a great chain. This chain is not like a blacksmith's chain. This chain is of the Lord's making. Whatever type of a chain God welds, by which He holds these evil, black, and foul demons in the abyss, it is this type of a chain that the angel uses against Satan.

3.  The Meaning of Satan's Four Names
    *   Satan is described here by four names. The names are in the same identical order as described in chapter 12. The first two names reflect his personality and the second two names are his actual, personal names. As most of us have two names, so Satan has two personal names.
    a.  *"Dragon"* refers to his beast-like leadership of the beast-like governments of the world.
    b.  *"Serpent"* refers to his subtle nature. In the beginning, in the garden of Eden, it was as a serpent that he manifested himself to our first parents and deflected them away from God.
    c.  *"Devil."* Although there are many demons, there is only one devil. Devil refers to his character as a liar and a murderer.

d. *"Satan,"* which means *"accuser."* He is the one who deceived our first parents. He is the one who brought death into the world. Satan is the enemy of God. He opposed God in the beginning. His works throughout Scripture are uncountable.

- God sent a mighty angel from heaven with a key and a mighty chain in his hand. That angel laid hold on that dragon, the serpent called the devil and Satan, and cast him into the abyss, where he set a seal upon him and shut him up in the bottomless pit.

4. The Words *"Pit"* and *"Hell"*

- The devil is cast into the pit, where he is bound a thousand years. But after a thousand years, he is loosed for a season, after which he is cast into the lake of fire and brimstone.

- The difference between the pit and the lake of fire is plainly stated in the Word of God.

- The lake of fire is hell. The pit is something else. The word *"pit,"* or "abyss," is used nine times in the New Testament, with seven of those instances being in Revelation. In Greek, it means "bottomless pit."

- We get a good idea of what it refers to when we read Luke 8:31. Look up this verse:

_____

_____

_____

_____

- The pit is a horrible place. It is an imprisonment; it is a place where demons, foul and wicked, are chained by the Lord God.

- It always refers to a place where fallen angels and foul and evil spirits are imprisoned by God. That is where Satan is going to be cast—chained, locked, and sealed for a thousand years.

- But there are other places beyond this life in the grave besides the pit, because we read in Revelation 19:20: *"And the beast was taken, and with him the false prophet…. These both were cast alive into the lake of fire burning with brimstone."* That is the ultimate place where the devil is cast, and we shall see that later.

- We shall see that the ultimate place of the antichrist, the false prophet, Satan, and the wicked dead shall eventually be in the same place.

- Some confusion exists about these two places, and that confusion lies in the translation—namely in the King James Version, because it translates the words *Sheol* and *Hades* as "hell." In these mistranslations, we come to a position of having no idea what God has revealed to us of that other world.

- The word *Sheol* is used in the Old Testament sixty-five times. Thirty-one times, in the Authorized Version, it is translated as *"hell."* Thirty-one times, it is translated as *"the grave."* Three times, it is translated as *"the pit."*

- In the New Testament, the word *Hades* is the exact equivalent of *Sheol* in the Old Testament. They are identical words. The word *"Hades"* in the New Testament is used eleven times. Ten times, it is translated as *"hell"*; once, it is translated as *"the grave."*

- But there is nothing in the words *Sheol* or *Hades* that refers to hell—nothing. All that *Sheol* means, and all that *Hades* means, is the departed, unseen world beyond this life.

5. The Millennium

- John sees an angel bind up Satan with chains and seal him in a pit. For one thousand years (the millennium), Satan will not be able to deceive humankind any longer. Ominously, though, Satan will be released at the end of the millennium one last time.

- Bible scholars differ over whether the one thousand years should be taken literally, but it seems clear that regardless of the actual length of time, the one thousand years describes a fixed amount of time determined by God. It begins when Satan is bound after the battle of Armageddon, and it ends when Satan is loosed for a season.

- John then describes an earthly kingdom that will be ruled by Christ and his saints. In particular, it is ruled by those saints who were martyred by the beast because of their allegiance to Christ. It is a new age, a new order. We cannot conceive of a world without sin in which righteousness reigns. Our lives have never known a time when we do not battle against sin and iniquity. Weeping, crying, separation, despair—these are common in our day. But in this Golden Age, they shall be taken away.

- Only the saved will enter the millennium, only those washed in the blood of the Lamb. No one who is not converted can enter. In Daniel 7:18, we read, *"But the saints of the most High shall take the kingdom, and possess the kingdom for ever, even for ever and ever."* Daniel repeats this emphasis again and again. All who enter the millennial kingdom are saved.

- *"And I saw the dead, small and great, stand before God; and the books were opened: and another book was opened, which is the book of life: and the dead were judged out of those things which were written in the books, according to their works"* (20:12).

- The millennial kingdom is not temporary. It is finally merged into the great final kingdom of the Lord God Almighty in the eternity of eternities. We are not to think that Christ comes into this world to establish a kingdom only for Satan to destroy it. Not so.

- God will give all believers throughout human history resurrected bodies to live, rule, and serve as priests with Christ in the millennium. Those who are resurrected will never die again; they will live forever with Christ.

- Also populating the earth during the millennium are those who were aligned with the beast before his demise and their descendants. They will live in their natural bodies under the rule of Christ and his resurrected saints during the millennium. Remember that only the antichrist's *armies* were killed in the battle of Armageddon.

6. After the Millennium

- We now come to a revelation in the Word of God that is hard for us to understand. After the millennium ends, Satan will be released from prison for a short period of time. He will deceive the people of the earth (not the resurrected saints).

- A leader called Gog, from a land called Magog, will gather a massive army and march on the city of Jerusalem, the city where Jesus lives and rules.

- The purpose of Satan's loosing is *"to gather them together to battle: the number of whom is as the sand of the sea"* (20:8). They war against the saints and all that God stands for.

- Why is Satan loosed? Many have speculated about this. Most say that it is so that all the people who grow up during the millennium, under the perfect and righteous reign of Christ, may have the chance to choose between good and evil, between God and Satan. These people have never been tempted or tried. Whether or not this is true, the thesis is plausible.

- I cannot fully explain why God allows the loosing of Satan, having placed him in the abyss. I don't understand this, but we know that every person who has been born must have a chance to choose between evil and good.

- Satan's release is only for a short season. Before he and his army can enter the city, God rains down fire on them, and they are all killed. God then throws Satan into the lake of fire with the beast and false prophet where they *"shall be tormented day and night for ever and ever"* (20:10).

- John has told us the fate of the beast, the false prophet, and of Satan himself. But what will happen to the people who, throughout human history, rejected God while they were alive, but are now deceased?

7. The White Throne

- John's vision moves to a great white throne upon which God sits. In verse 4, John says, *"And I saw thrones, and they sat upon them, and judgment was given unto them."*

- This is comparable to Daniel 7:9–10, 22: *"I beheld till the thrones were cast down, and the Ancient of days did sit, whose garment was white as snow, and the hair of his head like the pure wool.... Until the Ancient of days came, and judgment was given to the saints of the most High; and the time came that the saints possessed the kingdom."*

- The entire physical universe ceases to exist. All the unrighteous dead are resurrected and join the already resurrected believers. Both the saints and the wicked stand before God where He reviews the books which contain their deeds.

- John then mentions another book, the book of life. This book lists all the *saved* people of God. The only way for a person to be saved is through the blood of the Lamb of God, Jesus Christ. Every person whose name is not found in the book of life is sent to the lake of fire.

- The choice that confronts every human soul is the choice we must make for ourselves. No man can ever say that God sent him to hell. No man can ever say that God damned his soul. The fire was not made for man. It was made a torment and a fire and hell for the devil and his angels. The only people who are there are those who choose to cast their lot and their life and their destiny with the devil and his angels. There is no one there except those who choose to go. There is a choice for every man to make and it is found in verse 15: *"And whosoever was not found written in the book of life...."* This *"whosoever"* is the same word found in the great invitation of Revelation 22:17: *"Whosoever will, let him take the water of life freely."* It is the same *"whosoever"* found in John 3:16: *"Whosoever believeth in him should not perish, but have everlasting life."* God calls for an open confession of faith in which everyone can see, and anyone can know

- *"And death and hell were cast into the lake of fire. This is the second death"* (20:14). Death itself is also thrown into the lake of fire, meaning that no saved person will ever die again.

## How Much Do You Remember?

1. What are the meanings of Satan's four names?
2. What is the difference between the pit and the lake of fire?
3. Who are the only ones to enter with Christ into the millennium?
4. What happens to those whose names are not found in the book of life?
5. Why will those saved people never have to die again?

## Your Assignment for Next Week:

1. Read Revelation chapter 21.
2. Review your notes from this lesson.
3. Underline your Bible.

## Lesson 22 Notes

_____

_____

_____

_____

_____

_____

_____

_____

_____

_____

_____

_____

_____

_____

_____

_____

_____

_____

_____

<h1>Lesson 23</h1>
<h1>REVELATION 21</h1>

## A New Heaven—A New Earth—The New Jerusalem

After the great white throne judgment of Revelation 20, in Revelation 21, we come to the final climactic vision. Revelation 21:1–8 describes the new heaven and the new earth. Revelation 21:9–22 describes the holy city of God, the new Jerusalem.

The text speaks of recreation. This is a new, redeemed creation.

1. The New Heaven

   + The Bible speaks of three heavens: first, the atmospheric world in which we live—the heaven through which birds fly and clouds float; second, the heaven of the starry spheres, the milky way and all the stars you see at night; third, the heaven of heaves—the throne and dwelling place of God.

   + When the Bible says there is to be a new heaven, it refers certainly to the heaven immediately above us, the heaven of the atmosphere. I think it also includes the starry skies and all the systems that God has placed out here in space.

   + In the recreation of God, our entire universe will be remade in pristine glory.

2. The New Earth

   + John then says, *"I saw...a new earth"* (21:1).

   + Our sin-riddled planet is to experience a redemption and rejuvenation. No longer will it be torn by plows and hooks in order to yield an increase in its fruit. No longer will it be infected with thistles and thorns and briars. No longer will it be cut into graves and ploughed into cemeteries. No longer will it be moistened by tears or stained by the blood of man. There is to be a new, redeemed world. It is to be a paradise regained, Eden restored.

3. The New Jerusalem

   + *"And I John saw the holy city, new Jerusalem"* (21:2).

   + In the new creation, God is to build a new heavenly city as the center for His government, His people, and His dwelling place. Revelation 18 described the city of Babylon, the ultimate work of the hands of men, built in defiance of the Lord. This city will reflect the glory of the Lamb, a heavenly capital city for God.

   + It was the purpose of God that man should have dominion over the vast world around him. But sin cursed this dream and damned the life of man. But as far as sin is destroyed, just that far does redemption go. Because of sin, man was dispossessed of his rightful dominion, but by grace, God will restore to man the lost creation. Whatever sin has touched will be destroyed. God will redeem and cleanse.

   a. Not annihilation but renovation

      + In verse 1, John says, *"I saw a new heaven and a new earth: for the first heaven and the first earth were passed away."* Does this mean that the old, first heaven and the old, first earth were annihilated? Or does he mean that it is the same heaven renovated and redeemed, and that it is the same earth purified and regenerated?

      + The Greek word translated as *"passed away"* is *parerchomai*. Its primary meaning is not extinction or annihilation but refers to a change from one place or situation to another. For example, a ship would *parerchomai* through the sea, that is, "pass through" the sea and over the horizon. The ship "passes" over the horizon and is not seen anymore. It does not refer to the extinction or the annihilation of the ship. Likewise, when John says the first heaven and the first earth have passed away, he does not meant they have become extinct, but rather, that they have changed from one condition to another.

b. God's method of purification

♦ Isaiah 65:17 says, *"For, behold, I create new heavens and a new earth: and the former shall not be remembered, nor come into mind."* Everything that has been defiled by sin and Satan will be purified. It is the purification by fire that makes the earth and the heavens new.

♦ This method of purification is found in 2 Peter 3:7. Look at how the battle is fought in verse 20 and copy down this verse:

_____

_____

_____

_____

♦ Here, Peter gives us that probably is the most thorough description of how the Lord is going to create the new heavens and the new earth. It is one of the most advanced and scientific understandings of the composition of the earth and its final destruction found anywhere in Scripture. Its literal rendering should be as follows: "But the present heavens and earth are held in check by the same Word of God, stored up with fire, reserved unto the day of judgment and perdition of the ungodly." The statement "stored with fire" is to be found within the earth itself. We know this to be scientifically true, but Peter knew all this two thousand years ago. Isaiah new it twenty-five hundred years ago. God always knew it, for He is the one who made the earth.

♦ You will find in the promises of the World of God that we are to inherit the earth. Psalm 37:9 says, *"For evildoers shall be cut off: but those that wait upon the LORD, THEY SHALL INHERIT THE EARTH."* In Matthew 5:5, Jesus said, *"Blessed are the meek: for they shall inherit the earth."* Psalm 37:29 says, *"The righteous shall inherit the land, and dwell therein for ever."* When you compare these ideas, you come to one idea: God will make for us a new heaven and a new earth and a new city called the new Jerusalem.

4. Within the New City

♦ John first gives a description of the outside of the city, then he describes it from the inside.

♦ A description of the outside is recorded from verse 9–21. All the stones named are Greek words spelled out in English. The city radiates God's glory, which John compares to a brilliant jasper (likely a diamond in this case).

♦ John describes the inside of the city in verses 21 through verse 5 of chapter 22.

♦ Third, a high wall surrounds the city on four sides. On each wall are three gates (total of twelve), and twelve angels occupy the twelve gates. The gates have the names of the twelve tribes of Israel written on them. The wall of the city also has twelve foundations, and the names of the twelve apostles of Jesus are on the foundations. Twelve signifies completion and perfection and is the product of the sacred numbers three and four.

♦ What is the meaning of the walls, gates, angels, foundations, and names written on them? The wall is emphasized in 21:18, where we read it is made of jasper, meaning its purpose is not defense but rather radiating the glory of God. It is a great high wall because of the size of the city but especially due to the greatness of the glory of God. In keeping with verse 11, it had *"the glory of God."*

+ In verses 15–17, the angel measures the dimensions of the city. The city is constructed as a cube, with each dimension being twelve thousand furlongs (about 1,500 miles), a truly enormous volume. The walls are 144 cubits (216 feet) thick.

+ To emphasize the glory of the city, John writes that the walls are made of jasper (a precious stone), and the city is made of a clear gold. No such gold is known, so John must be attempting to describe a precious metal that is beyond human experience.

+ In short, Revelation builds on a lengthy tradition in depicting the majesty of the celestial city yet transforms these images into a description of the glory the saints will receive on the basis of the presence of God and their priestly status in the eternal city.

+ Verse 22 records the fact that there is no temple in the new Jerusalem, because God the Father and Jesus are the temple. The glorious light that shines forth from God and His Son means that there is no need for the sun or moon in the sky.

+ In reflecting upon the glories of the new Jerusalem, perhaps John was overwhelmed by the vision of the presence of God and recalled the prophecy of Isaiah 60:19: *"The sun shall be no more thy light by day; neither for brightness shall the moon give light unto thee: but the Lord shall be unto thee an everlasting light, and thy God thy glory."*

+ Unlike typical cities, the gates of New Jerusalem will never close. All the kings of the earth will be welcome to the city to honor God. But, John reminds us, only those whose names are written in the book of life will enter the city. Evil will never stain the new heaven and new earth.

+ In Revelation 22:1–2, we see that the new Jerusalem is also the restored garden of Eden. *"And he shewed me a pure river of water of life, clear as crystal, proceeding out of the throne of God and of the Lamb. In the midst of the street of it, and on either side of the river, was there the tree of life"* (22:2). There is a river of life that flows directly from the throne of God the Father and the Lamb. Note that it's a single throne that they share.

+ The curse from Genesis 3:14 is reversed because sin is no more. All of God's servants will worship Him in the restored Eden, and they will worship Him face-to-face.

+ The presence of the river of life in the new Jerusalem is a picturesque way of saying that death, with all its baleful accompaniments, has been abolished and that life reigns supreme

+ There, the servants of God will reign with Him forever and ever.

## How Much Do You Remember?

1. What are the three heavens referred to in the Bible?
2. What is it important that the new earth and new heaven are a regeneration and not an annihilation?
3. Why is there no physical temple in the new Jerusalem?
4. Why is it important that the new Jerusalem should be compared to the garden of Eden?

## Your Assignment for Next Week:

1. Read Revelation chapter 22.
2. Review your notes from this lesson.
3. Underline your Bible.

## Lesson 23 Notes

_____

_____

_____

_____

_____

_____

_____

_____

_____

_____

_____

_____

_____

_____

_____

_____

_____

_____

_____

_____

_____

# Lesson 24
# REVELATION 22

Alpha and Omega—The Last Invitation—The Words of This Prophecy—The Last Promise in the Bible

1. The Alpha and the Omega (verses 12–13, 16)

   * Four times in the book of Revelation we read the words: *"I am Alpha and Omega."*

   * The first occurrence is found in Revelation 1:8 where we read: *"I am Alpha and Omega, the beginning and the ending, saith the Lord, which is, and which was, and which is to come, the Almighty."*

   * The second time this expression is used is in this same chapter, verses 10 and 11: *"I was in the Spirit on the Lord's day, and heard behind me a great voice, as of a trumpet, saying, I am Alpha and Omega, the first and the last: and, What thou seest, write in a book, and send it unto the seven churches…."* Here, Christ says he is the Lord of time and of history. All the unfolding ages are in His hands.

   * The third time we read this expression is in Revelation 21:5–6: *"And he that sat upon the throne said, Behold, I make all things new* [a new heaven, a new earth, a new capital city]*…. I am Alpha and Omega, the beginning and the end."* Here, He states that He is the Lord God of the new order and of the new creation.

   * The last and fourth time this expression is used is here in Revelation 22:12–13: *"And, behold, I come quickly; and my reward is with me, to give every man according as his work shall be. I am Alpha and Omega, the beginning and the end, the first and the last."* It is affirmed of our Lord Christ that He is the judge of all men. He is the great judge of the earth and He sits in jurisdiction of time, history, and creation.

   * All four of these passages are affirmation of the deity of our Lord Christ.

   * An affirmation of the deity of our Lord is also found in Revelation 22:16: *"I am the root and the off-spring of David."* The phrase *"the offspring of David"* is a reference to His genealogical descent from the great king of Israel.

   * Notice that the text first says, *"I am the root…of David".* That identical expression is used in Revelation 5:5: *"And one of the elders saith unto me, Weep not: behold, the Lion of the tribe of Judah, the Root of David, hath prevailed to open the book, and to loose the seven seals thereof."*

   * Notice those words, *"the Root of David"*—a tree grows from its root. The root is first, and afterward, the sprout and the trunk. This saying, therefore, is an avowal that our Lord Christ was before David. In Isaiah 11:10, He is called *"the root of Jesse."* He existed before both of them—their spiritual life was derived from Him.

   * The Lord said, *"Before Abraham was, I am"* (John 8:58). Before Jesse, before David, the great God Almighty existed.

   * In Isaiah 9:6 we find a beautiful passage that marvelously prefigures this expression. Look up this verse:

   _____

   _____

   _____

   _____

- That child that was born is the eternal Word in the flesh. This son that is given to the everlasting Father in the person and presence of a child is the offspring of Mary. In the providence of God, and in the fullness of time, the Lord God descended from heaven, wrapped Himself in human flesh in the womb of a virgin girl, and offered Himself as a sacrifice for our sins in the body God prepared for Him. Through the atonement of His blood, our iniquities and transgressions are washed away.

- A few other Scriptures that depict the eternal existence and the immutability of the Lord Christ: Hebrews 1:10–12, John 8:58, Colossians 1:17, Hebrews 1:3, and John 1:1–3.

  a. The Alpha and Omega of Scriptures

    - Our Lord is not only the Alpha and Omega, the beginning and the end, the revelation of the existence and the being and the person of deity, but He is also the Alpha and Omega of the Holy Scriptures.

    - The entire Bible is a revelation about Him. From the first verse Genesis until the last benediction, when the grace of our Lord Jesus Christ is bestowed upon all of us, He is the great alphabet of the entire story, the Alpha and Omega.

  b. The Alpha and Omega of Honor and Exaltation

    - If there is any reference to the high and holy majesty in the Bible, it is of Him.

    - If there is any description of a prophetic office or a priestly character, its ultimate example can be found in Him.

    - All other prophets follow after Him, for He is the great High Priest making atonement for the souls of His people. He is the King of Kings and of His dominion there is no end.

  c. The Alpha and Omega of Worship and Devotion

    - He is the beginning and the end of all exultation and glory.

    - In Philippians 2:9–11, we see these words:

      > Wherefore God also hath highly exalted him, and given him a name which is above every name: that at the name of Jesus every knee should bow, of things in heaven, and things in earth, and things under the earth; and that every tongue should confess that Jesus Christ is Lord, to the glory of God the Father.

  d. The Alpha and Omega of Our Salvation

    - What is it to be saved? It is to be saved by the Lord Jesus. What is it to be a Christian? It is to be a follower of the Lord Jesus.

    - Jesus said, "I am Alpha and Omega, the beginning and the end. I will give unto him that is athirst of the fountain of the water of life freely" (Revelation 21:6).

    - Whatever there is in our lives, He is there to cleanse, to forgive, to wash away, and to make us clean, because He is the Alpha and Omega of our salvation.

2. The Last Invitation (Revelation 22:17)

  - This part of the lesson is based around one word—"come."

  - Sometimes, in this epilogue of the book of Revelation, different voices are heard. Sometimes it is the voice of John, sometimes the voice of the angel, and sometimes a deeper voice from the throne—the Lord God speaking.

  - Sometimes it is difficult amidst the translation to tell which one is speaking, as it is here in this verse: "And the Spirit and the bride say, Come. And let him that heareth say, Come. And let him that is athirst come. And whosoever will, let him take the water of life freely" (Revelation 22:17).

♦ The first three times we see the word *"come,"* it is an answering cry to the significant, triumphant messages of our Lord, who announced in verse 12 of this same chapter, *"Behold, I come quickly."*

♦ The first voices of the text—the voice of the Spirit, the voice of the bride of Christ, the voice of him that heareth (each individual member of the congregation)—are those who reply to the sublime announcement of our Lord, who says, *"Behold, I come quickly."* They say, and we say, "Come, Lord, come."

♦ Then the Lord's voice is heard again, remembering the lost and thirsty of this weary world, when Jesus extends the invitation for all of those who might be thirsty to come to Him: *"And whosoever will, let him take the water of life freely"* (22:17).

♦ So we shall speak of this in two parts—first, the reply of the Spirit, the church, and of the individual hearer to the sublime announcement of the living Christ that He will come quickly; second, we shall speak of the pathos in the voice of our blessed Lord as He encourages the thirsty and the willing to come and to drink of the water of life.

a. The voice of the Spirit, church, and individual hearer

♦ It is natural for those of us who are Christians to join in with those of this passage and say, "Come, Lord Jesus, Come." The longing and the desire of the Holy Spirit of God is to exalt the Lord Jesus Christ—to reveal Him in beauty, glory, and triumph. When the Lord announces, *"Behold, I come quickly,"* our spirit replies, "Come, Lord, Come".

♦ The bride says, "Come"; that is the bride of Christ, and they repeat the invitation. The bride of Christ, His church, throughout all ages and centuries, has been in prayer, waiting for the coming of the Lord. However different groups may interpret His coming, the true church of Christ is ever moved by that prayer of appeal: "Thy kingdom come; thy will be done."

♦ If the church is filled with the Holy Spirit, and if the Holy Spirit speaks through his church, they have a common prayer, and that is that the Lord will come again. The church cries in the Spirit, and the Spirit prays and cries in the church, for the appearance of our blessed Lord and Savior, Jesus Christ.

♦ *"And let him that heareth say, Come"* (22:17). At the sublime announcement of our Lord, *"Behold, I come quickly,"* let every individual member of the congregation come, and let every member of the household of faith when he hears the word that is read and the Revelation that is delivered, let him say in his heart, "Yes, Lord Jesus. Come back."

♦ That is the token of the born again Christian. No unsaved man longs for the return of the Savior. To him, it is the day of judgment and foreboding, and it is the day of damnation. But to us who belong to Him, it is a blessed thing.

b. The voice of the Lord

1.) *"Come."*

♦ Second, in the midst of the answering cry of the Spirit, the bride, and the individual Christ, the Lord speaks loudly and clearly when He says, *"And let him that is athirst come. And whosoever will, let him take the water of life freely"* (22:17). It is as though the Lord says to the unsaved individual, "Let Me make one last appearance to you, that you might come."

♦ The word *"come"* is a favorite of the Lord throughout the Bible.

♦ In the face of terrible judgment of the flood, the Lord commanded Noah to build an ark, and when he had built it, He said to Noah, *"Come thou and all thy house into the ark"* (Genesis 7:1). The great lawgiver, Moses, standing in the midst of the camp among his people, and they being in an orgy of sin, said, *"Who is on* the LORD'S SIDE? LET HIM COME UNTO ME" (Exodus 32:26). It is the message of the gospel of the Old Testament in Isaiah 1:18, which says, *"Come now, and let us reason together."* Or, in Isaiah 55:1, which says, *"Ho, everyone that thirsteth, come ye to the waters…yea, come, buy wine and milk without money and without price."*

- ✦ The word *"come"* was the constant word of invitation on the lips of our Savior. Passing by the sea, He saw the first disciples fishing, and said, *"Come ye after me"* (Mark 1:17). The Lord also said, *"Suffer little children to come unto me, and forbid them not"* (Luke 18:16).

- ✦ This is the climactic purpose of every worship service, of every gospel sermon, and of all the teaching that we do. It is for people to come to the Lord Jesus. A preacher needs only the simple sermon, "Come, come to the Lord Jesus. Come and be saved."

2.) *"Whosoever"*

- ✦ We have now arrived at the last, most inclusive summation of all the invitations of God in all of the Word of God when we read, *"And whosoever will, let him take of the water of life freely"* (22:17).

- ✦ The word *"whosoever"* includes everybody; every soul. The whosoever will include everyone—if I elect, God elects; if I will, God wills.

- ✦ *"And whosoever will"*—the condition is not with God, it is not with Christ, the condition lies in me. God says, *"whosoever will."*

- ✦ Notice that little word, *"let."* Whosoever will, *let* him. There is significant meaning in that word. When God says, *"Let him"*— where is the power that can interdict God's mandate?

3.) *"Take"*

- ✦ *"Whosoever will, let him **take** the water of life freely."*

- ✦ *"Let him **take**,"* and I emphasize again, *take*. What a simple gospel; what a simple message. Let him take.

- ✦ Does a man desire Christ? Then let him take Christ. Does a man desire life? Then let him take life. Does a mean desire heaven? Then let him take heaven.

- ✦ God instructs all of us to tell those who need salvation, *"Let him take."* There is no word about feelings, about carrying a load of righteousness and good works—God just simply says, *"let him take,"* and that's it.

- ✦ God says grace, abounding grace, will provide the repentance, the faith, and the gifts that bring us night unto God. Do not bring price, cost, good works, commendations, or recommendations. Just accept what God has to offer by *taking* Him.

3.  Can God's People Be Removed from the Book of Life? (verses 18–19)

*If any man shall add unto these things, God shall add unto him the plagues that are written in this book: and if any man shall take away from the words of the book of this prophecy, God shall take away his part out of the book of life, and out of the holy city, and from the things which are written in this book.*

(Revelation 22:18-19)

- ✦ Having been saved and regenerated, can one fall away from the grace and keeping of our Lord?

- The answer is plain to me. This passage is not discussing the possibility of the saved being ultimately lost; it is but a warning from God that His Word is immutable, eternal, and unchangeable.

- This is a serious and solemn mandate from the Lord, that His Word is not to be changed, mutilated, or impaired. It is not to be added to and it is not to be taken away from.

- What, then, is the meaning of this threat, that if any man take away from the book, God will take his name out of the book of life? Does it mean that a man who is regenerated and born again could fall away and finally be lost?

- That is impossible. It is as impossible as is the suggestion that a regenerated man would mutilate God's Holy Word. He would not do that. It does not belong to the elect of God to change God's Word, nor would it enter the heart of a man who was regenerated to do God's Word that way.

## How Much Do You Remember?

1. What do the four occurrences of *"I am Alpha and Omega"* affirm?
2. What three words signify the voice of the Lord in this chapter?
3. Once saved and regenerated, can one fall away from God?

## Lesson 24 Notes

_____

_____

_____

_____

_____

_____

_____

_____

_____

_____

_____

_____

_____

_____

_____

_____

_____

_____

_____

_____

_____

_____

_____

_____

_____

_____

_____

# Lesson 25
# A SUMMATION OF THE BOOK OF REVELATION

As we look at this prophecy once again from a lofty mountain, we shall see a brief overall panorama of what we have learned throughout our course of study. So we shall take an exalted place by the side of our Lord and, with Him, look over the vista of this apocalypse—this unveiling.

1. The Book Itself

   + Without the apocalypse, the Bible would be incomplete. However great and broad the base, without the capstone of the apocalypse, it is forever unfinished and incomplete. Without this final and climactic vision, the great issues raised in Scripture are forever unresolved and unanswered.

   + The vision was given to a man named John. Three times He calls his name John. He says, in Revelation 1:4, *"John to the seven churches which are in Asia."* Then, in Revelation 1:9, *"I John, who also am your brother, and companion in tribulation, and in the kingdom and patience of Jesus Christ, was in the isle that is called Patmos, for the word of God, and for the testimony of Jesus Christ."* In Revelation 22:8, in the epilogue, he said, *"I John saw these things, and heard them."*

   a. Who is John?

      + He is a man of such authority in the churches that his word is immediately accepted as the Word of God himself.

      + He is the apostle John and he had such an unusual place and prominence among those early Christians.

      + When John left the city of Jerusalem during the Judean War, he came to the Roman province of Asia around A.D. 69 He became pastor of the church at Ephesus and the spiritual leader for all of God's people in that part of the eastern Roman Empire.

      + Domitian reigned as emperor of the Roman Empire from A.D. 81 until about A.D. 96 Thus, the revelation was seen on the Isle of Patmos about A.D. 96, after John was exiled to that island for the Word of God.

      + Clement of Alexandria, another father of the early church, said that after the death of Domitian, John left his exile in Patmos and returned to Ephesus, so the vision was seen and written down about A.D. 96.

   b. The apocalypse

      + The word *"apocalypse"* is found in the first sentence of the book of Revelation. Your Bible says, *"The Revelation of Jesus Christ,"* which is the apocalypse, or, translated literally, the unveiling and uncovering of Jesus Christ.

      + The book of Revelation is the uncovering of Christ's deity, revealing Him as Lord over all.

      + Twenty-eight times, He is called *"the Lamb of God"*—a reference to His humanity, but many times, He is worshipped in heaven as God.

      + The apocalypse is a book of prophecy. Four times, it is called just that. (See Revelation 1:3; 22:10, 18, 19.)

      + There are seven beatitudes in the book of Revelation, which we covered in an earlier lesson, but this one says, *"Blessed is he that readeth, and they that hear the words"* (Revelation 1:3).

- The book was written to be read publicly and privately. There is a blessing for both the one who reads it and for the congregation that reads it.

- The New Testament has one volume of prophecy and it comprises God's answer to the question of the ages, when we consider the great promise of our Lord: *"and if I go and prepare a place for you, I will come again"* (John 14:3).

- Is that promise never to be fulfilled? This book of prophecy is God's answer to that tremendous prayer of His people, "Thy kingdom come." It is the unveiling, the open vision, of the coming of our triumphant Christ.

2. The Outline of Revelation

- The vision follows an outline given to us in Revelation 1:19, which we have covered but will review briefly.

  a. First, God's outline says, *"Write the things which thou hast seen,…."*

     - John wrote down the vision that he had seen, the vision of the glorified Lord recorded in the first chapter of the Revelation.

  b. Then, the Lord says, *"and the things which are,…."*

     - John belonged to the same dispensation of grace in which we live, the era of the churches. The *"things which are"* refers to the things of the churches.

     - So John wrote down, in the second division of things which are, the course of the churches.

     - There is the Ephesian period—the days of the apostles.

     - There is the Smyrnan period—the days of the martyrs.

     - There is the Pergamian period—the days when the church was married to the state.

     - There is the Thyatirian period—the days when the church was dressed in purple and bedecked as the woman Jezebel.

     - There is the Sardian period—the days when great men of faith called the people back to the true faith.

     - There is the Philadelphian period—the days when the church of the great missionary movements seeking to bring the name of Jesus to the whole world.

     - Finally, there is the Laodicean period—the days when the doors of the church have been closed.

  c. The third thing the Lord told John to write was *"the things which shall be hereafter."*

     - When we come to Revelation 4:1, we find those same words used again: *"After this I looked, and, behold, a door was opened in heaven: and the first voice which I heard was as it were of a trumpet talking with me; which said, Come up hither, and I will shew thee things which must be hereafter* [things that must be after these things]".

     - Revelation 3 closes the church age. Revelation 4 marks the opening of the vista that lies beyond the rapture of God's people. They are not seen any longer here on the earth. The bride of Christ is in heaven.

     - In Revelation 19, the bride of Christ, after her marriage to the Lamb, and after the marriage supper of the Lamb, is seen coming in glory with her triumphant Lord.

     - How did the people of the church get up there? They were taken up. The old Anglo-Saxon word is *raptured*, which means taken away or snatched away.

     - John is taken up into heaven, and there, he sees the raptured church and the throne, and around the throne, the four and twenty elders.

d. Chapters 4–21

  + The chapters that follow in the third great division of the Revelation are, by the Spirit of God, a revelation, a disclosure of the days spoken of by our Lord in the apocalyptic discourse in Matthew 24.

  + It is the vision of the awesome days before Christ comes again to the earth.

  + Chapters 4–5 prepare us for the book of redemption placed in the blessed hands of our Lord.

  + Chapter 6 describes the first six seals.

  + Chapter 7 recounts the sealing of God's witnesses, twelve thousand from each one of the tribes of Israel.

  + Chapter 8 records the opening of the seventh seal and the blowing of the first four trumpets.

  + Chapter 9 describes the sounding of the fifth and sixth trumpets.

  + Chapter 10 follows the story of the little book given to John, that he might understand the bitter judgments of God upon the unbelieving.

  + Chapter 11 records two great witnesses of the Lord, and finally, the blowing of the seventh and final trumpet.

  + Beginning with chapter 12, God reviews the great personages in the final denouement. There is the woman who gave birth to the man child who is to rule the earth with the rod of iron. This woman is Israel, who gave birth to the Savior, the Christ. There is the devil, that old dragon, ready to destroy the Lord and His people. There is Michael, who stands up for God's people against Satan. After Michael's victorious war in heaven, Satan is flung down to the earth like a sensor with its fire blazing and burning. Thus, in thunder and lightning, the judgments of God fall in the final days to the earth.

  + In chapter 13, there is the disclosure of the two final earth systems, the political system headed by one beast and the religious system headed by the false prophet.

  + Chapter 14 brings to view God's people who are saved in those awesome days of tribulation. In the beginning days of the tribulation, God seals 144,000, and in chapter 14, we find that there are not 143,999 but 144,000 still preserved because they are the elect of God. Also in chapter 14 is the great revelation of the harvest of the earth, which no man could number.

  + Chapters 15–16 are the pouring out of the last vials of wrath.

  + Chapter 17 describes the judgment upon that false religious system called Jezebel, or Babylon.

  + Chapter 18 is the judgment of God upon men who worship mammon, money, or commercial Babylon.

  + Chapter 19 is the coming of Christ. In the midst of the fearful battle of Armageddon, when it looks as though men will destroy one another, the heavens open and the Lord returns with His people, as Jude describes: *"Behold, the Lord cometh with ten thousands of his saints."* (Jude 1:14).

  + Chapter 20 is the binding of Satan and the millennium days.

  + Chapter 21 brings the new creation. There is a new heaven, a new earth, and a new Jerusalem, where there is no more sadness, crying, tears, sorrow, or death.

3. The Last Promise in the Book (chapter 22:20–21)

  + We come now to the closing and final thought of our study of the book of Revelation.

  + These two verses, verses 20 and 21, close the cannon of the Holy Scripture.

- *"He which testifieth these things saith, Surely I come quickly. Amen. Even so, come, Lord Jesus. The grace of our Lord Jesus Christ be with you all. Amen."* And the book is closed. The book is then closed forever. It shall not be added to nor taken away from.

- These verses are the final time Christ speaks in the earth. The next time we hear the voice of the Son of man will be when He descends in glory with a shout and with a voice of the archangel and with the trump of God.

- These last few words of Scripture are so full of the truth of God, as though the Holy Spirit did sum up in these few words the whole revelation and testimony of the Lord through the ages.

- First, the certainty of His coming. Second, the last words of a Man, the affirmation and the last prayer that fell from the lips of Him. And third, you see the final benediction remembrance of the love and the grace of the Lord Jesus upon His people.

- *"Surely I come quickly."* This is an avowal of the certainty of our Lord's return. This has been the text and the theme of the apocalypse throughout the entire book.

- The Bible opens with a promise of a coming Lord. The Holy Spirit closes the Scripture with a promise of the coming again of our Lord.

- In Genesis 3:15, God said that He would present a seed of the woman that would cause a conflict that would last forever and forever between the Lord and Satan.

- The one who is coming again is the one who said, *"If I go and prepare a place for you, I will come again, and receive you unto myself; that where I am, there ye may be also"* (John 14:3).

- That same one of whom the angel said, *"Ye men of Galilee, why stand ye gazing up into heaven? this same Jesus, which is taken up from you into heaven, shall so come in like manner"* (Acts 1:11).

- Paul said, *"For the Lord himself shall descend from heaven"* (1 Thessalonians 4:16).

- Thus, when we read this statement, *"Surely I come quickly,"* the word *"I"* means the blessed Lord and Savior Jesus Christ.

- And now the final benediction: *"The grace of our Lord Jesus Christ be with you all. Amen"* (Revelation 22:21).

## How Much Do You Remember?

1. What are the three main divisions of the book of Revelation?
2. Write a paragraph detailing how you've grown spiritually through completing this course of study and what new knowledge you have gained.

## Lesson 25 Notes

_____

_____

_____

_____

_____

_____

_____

_____

_____

_____

_____

_____

_____

_____

_____

_____

_____

_____

_____

_____

_____

_____

_____

_____

# ABOUT THE AUTHOR

Dr. Alan B. Stringfellow (1922–1993), a Bible teacher and minister of the gospel for more than four decades, specialized in Christian education. Long concerned with the struggle most people have in understanding the Bible, he set out to write a study course that would bring believers more knowledge and a greater appreciation of God's Word. He wrote *Through the Bible in One Year*, *Great Truths of the Bible*, and *Great Characters in the Bible* for laymen, to be taught by laymen. Dr. Stringfellow trained at Southwestern Baptist Theological Seminary in Fort Worth, Texas, after which he served at Travis Avenue Baptist Church in Fort Worth; First Baptist Church of West Palm Beach, Florida; First Baptist Church of Fresno, California; and First Baptist Church of Van Nuys, California.